Build Rapid Expertise:
How to Learn Faster, Acquire Knowledge More Thoroughly, Comprehend Deeper, and Reach a World-Class Level

By Peter Hollins, Author and Researcher at petehollins.com

Table of Contents

CHAPTER 1. ACCELERATE YOUR EXPERTISE — 7

- THE MYTH OF EXPERTISE — 9
- THE BIOLOGY OF EXPERTISE — 15

CHAPTER 2. HOW TO FIND, INTAKE, AND UNDERSTAND INFO BETTER AND FASTER — 31

- THE RESEARCH PROCESS FROM A TO Z — 32
- NEXT-LEVEL READING AND CONSUMPTION — 45

CHAPTER 3. UNLIMITED MEMORY — 65

- HOW MEMORY WORKS — 67
- SPACED REPETITION — 72
- CHUNKING — 78
- RETRIEVAL PRACTICE — 82
- CHANGE LOCATIONS — 89
- CONSTRUCT VIVID IMAGERY — 93
- CREATE A STORY — 96
- MIND MAPPING — 99

CHAPTER 4. PATHS FOR GAINING EXPERTISE — 105

- FOLLOW THE LEADER — 106
- BECOME THE MINIMUM VIABLE EXPERT (MVE) — 118
- ABIDE BY BLOOM — 126

CHAPTER 5. MINDSET OF THE EXPERT — 137

- REALISTIC EXPECTATIONS — 138
- CRITICAL THINKING — 146
- YOU KNOW NOTHING — 155
- THE ONE PROBLEM WITH EXPERTISE … — 166

CHAPTER 6. EXPERTISE REARS ITS HEAD — 175

- LEARNING A LANGUAGE — 176
- LEARNING A MUSICAL INSTRUMENT — 184
- LOOK LIKE AN EXPERT — 191
- CATCH OTHERS PRETENDING TO BE EXPERTS — 199

SUMMARY GUIDE — 207

Chapter 1. Accelerate Your Expertise

The concept of expertise is something of a moving target in our modern age. Many people only want to grant the title of "expert" to someone who has earned a doctorate in a certain subject, with everyone else needing to defer. Others assert that expertise is the opposite of academic knowledge, and instead comes from firsthand experience—so-called *street smarts*. Luckily for us, the reality is a mix of both of these. Expertise can be granted, earned, or bestowed in any number of ways, which is a relief for those of us wanting to cultivate more of it for ourselves.

However we define expertise, it's clear that we all desire it. We know it's something that has the power to command respect and attention. We think that if we have enough of the right kind of expertise, it can change our lives and make us rich. This leads us to sometimes think that if we *don't* have expertise in something useful, our lives will be meaningless and empty. And so on. The way we think about skill, competence and talent can bring us to our highest highs and lowest lows. Regardless of whether or not this particular vision is true, the importance of having *an expertise* (or two) can certainly move you forward in life in tangible ways.

Let's break down what expertise actually is, for the purposes of this book. Expertise can generally be defined as the **mastery** over a certain field, skill, or topic. A bartender is an expert on alcoholic drinks and small talk with customers, while a pianist is an expert on musical rhythm and hand-eye coordination. A construction worker is an expert in working with power tools and estimating amounts of lumber and cement. It doesn't matter if people have acquired their expertise intentionally or as a byproduct; their skills help all the same.

You may not yet be an expert on what you want, but that's what this book is for. It's to take you from Point A to Point B, where Point A is the initial awareness of an intriguing topic, and Point B is a level of mastery that outpaces that of 99.9 percent of the population. Surprisingly, this process is easier than you might imagine it to be. As you just read with the bartenders and pianists, gaining expertise doesn't necessarily have to follow a set path.

Also notably, you don't need to be an Einstein-level genius to achieve the type of expertise you want, and to start experiencing the benefits in your own life. Finally, as you read, you will hopefully be convinced that you already possess a good degree of mastery – or at least the seeds of mastery. In this introductory chapter on accelerating your expertise, we'll cover one of the most important mindsets for learning, and the biological basis of expertise.

The Myth of Expertise

Myth and misconception is a handy starting point in our preliminary discussion of expertise, in particular the cultural notion of inborn genius. The myth of innate intelligence being the ultimate ceiling for our potential is a harmful belief that has been propagated over through the years. Think of depictions of genius in movies or the media, and how often it's portrayed as automatic, easy and a foregone conclusion. The myth is that you simply have to be smart to start with, and if you're not, you'll never achieve the expertise you want. The myth also tells us that inborn intelligence is more important than hard work, perseverance, and effort.

Talent and innate intelligence can help, of course, but your *attitude* about learning is far more important when it comes to true expertise. Why? Because if you believe your abilities are fixed in place and cannot really be altered, you'll put up mental blocks that hinder your learning. Why bother trying to be better when you can't, right?

These mental blocks, and this overall myth, create a *fixed mindset*. Have you ever heard anyone say, *"I can't draw,"* or *"I'm not good at sports,"* or *"I could never do that?"* These statements are said with a degree of resignation and an attitude that suggests the current state of affairs is permanent and completely out of that person's control. Each statement reveals a subtle way that our thoughts affect our actions. All of these are examples of a fixed mindset, of people who believe abilities are set in stone... and therefore don't spend any effort improving them. It's a self-fulfilling prophesy, though, and the belief actually *does* come true. The tragedy of this mindset is that it convinces people not to take the time to practice, or to work through and puzzle over something enough to actually acquire a new skill.

Take me, for instance. I used to think I'd never be able to draw. The way I understood the world was that there were artists, and then there were other people. I just so happened to be one of those unlucky "other people." I had my own areas of creativity, but drawing wasn't one of them.

For years, I carried around a belief about innate talent that meant, in my mind, I'd never be able to draw. It completely prevented me from even trying, though I would have loved to take art classes when I was younger. Because I thought that no matter the effort I put into drawing, I'd never produce work I was happy with, I decided to focus on the areas where my natural talents were. Imagine my surprise when, just a couple of years ago, I finally signed up for an art class at a local community college, and I was one of the best students in the class!

The fixed mindset is harmful because it keeps you from taking even the first step. However, according to psychologist and researcher Carol Dweck, mindset is something that we can change. People tend to fall into one of two predictable patterns as they go through life: they stay mired in the fixed mindset we've talked about, or they adopt a more adaptable and useful *growth mindset*.

The big difference with this mindset is that talent and ability are not seen as fixed and inborn, but rather something that could potentially develop with time and effort. A growth mindset believes that challenges are opportunities, and that failure is a chance for growth. If there is effort, then there will be some tangible reward; all things are attainable. Rather than seeking out evidence that proves they're not smart, people with a growth mindset focus on pursuing process and progress, searching out opportunities to stretch their existing abilities. In other words, where a fixed mindset person would give up immediately and say, "I'm just not good at it," a growth mindset person would say "I'm not good at it *yet*, but I will *be* after working at it!"

You can probably already see the difference that this attitude would make to your day-to-day life. This belief that intelligence and talent can be developed over time has profound consequences for our quest for expertise – for a start, it allow you to embark on a quest in the first place! Believing that your qualities are carved in stone (the fixed mindset) creates constant shutdowns and dead ends.

People with this mindset will avoid difficult situations, refuse to challenge themselves, and effectively evaluate every situation to see whether it will make them look smart or dumb, or whether they will succeed or fail. After all, if you can't improve, why subject yourself to the discomfort of constantly making efforts and failing? And because this mindset sees ability as a personal attribute rather than an action one takes, failing creates an unacceptable wound to the ego. And in that case, it's better to attempt only those tasks you can be guaranteed to succeed at! It's a recipe for stagnation.

In contrast, believing that the hand you're dealt is just the starting point for development (the growth mindset) creates possibility: it means that you believe that your basic skills can be can cultivated through effort. So, you make that effort. A person with a growth mindset embodies a passion for learning. Often, the person we assume is a naturally gifted genius is actually not someone who was handed their competence for free, but worked hard for it.

The growth mindset ties neatly into learning. If you are struggling with learning, you have two choices. You can either subscribe to a fixed mindset and give up, saying "Learning just isn't what I'm good at," or you can follow a growth mindset and say "I just haven't put in enough time and effort yet, I'll work until I figure it out! It's possible!"

Growth mindsets prioritize and even cherish challenge. People with a growth mindset know that:

- Trying and failing is part of the process; in fact, attempts and failures are the best teachers you will ever have
- Learning requires stumbling, correcting, and growing – which doesn't mean you're a failure or a bad person, or that you should give up
- You don't have to know everything in advance to succeed eventually
- Practice and skill-building are more important than inborn talent

- You're always a beginner, which means you can always grow and improve
- Results aren't important; the process is
- Effort is the important part; the outcome you want only comes with the corresponding input

You can see how these factors contribute to a mindset for learning and expertise. Try to embody those statements and set the correct expectations for yourself. No one is brilliant or perfect in their first go-round, and everyone struggles with different things. Many people struggle with everything. It is only through hard work and effort that *anyone* ever improves at anything, and this is certainly how it is to learn new information and material.

If you believe you can do it, you will probably be able to do it. Even if you struggle, you still begin and will likely find yourself in a better position than if you had merely given up. If you don't believe you can do it, you are probably wasting your time. That is the importance of the growth mindset, not just in learning and growing expertise. Struggle is all part of the process.

All this boils down to the proposition that you can indeed learn whatever you want, no matter what you think of yourself. There are people out there who are more intelligent, wealthier and luckier than you – but it won't matter if they are unwilling to take action, to put in the effort, and to learn. Your IQ or the education level of your parents is not nearly as important as your attitude and beliefs toward learning.

There is a saying that "hard work beats talent until talent starts working hard." At the very least, we can control half of that equation—the part about working hard. Experts are made, not born. If you have lofty ideas of how unattainable expertise is, now is the time to challenge them and see expertise as something that is completely within your grasp. We instinctively know that humanity does not operate within a caste system, so why should our pursuit for knowledge function any differently?

The Biology of Expertise

Expertise, learning, and the ability to quickly get from Point A to Point B in terms of knowledge is something to be understood on a neurological level. What's happening in our brains that allows such a process, and how can we use this knowledge to help us?

This topic begins with the concept of neuroplasticity, which is the degree to which our brains are malleable and shapeable, much like a mound of clay. It's a positive aspect that allows our brains to develop and grow, and it's what allows babies and children to be the learning machines they are. Neuroplasticity, also known as brain plasticity, is a term that refers to the brain's ability to change and adapt as a result of experience. That last bit is important – the brain only adapts in response to changes in the environment, i.e. challenge and effort.

Up until the 1960s, experts and scientists believed that changes in the brain could only take place during infancy and childhood. It was thought that by early adulthood, the brain's physical structure was mostly permanent, i.e. that the mound of clay would eventually harden and stay the same shape forever. In other words, the fixed mindset was the assumption.

Modern research, however, has demonstrated that the brain continues to create new neural pathways and alter existing ones in order to adapt to new experiences, learn new information, and create new memories. After all, the human brain consists of over 86 billion neurons, and these neurons can create multiple new pathways as a result of fresh knowledge and experience. There has even been new research to suggest that brain neurons can regenerate in a limited set of circumstances. This means that we can see the growth mindset reflected *physiologically* in the brain, which is not a fixed organ, but one that grows and adapts with us.

Learning and expertise can be said to occur neurologically in two primary ways. The first is through funneling information into our long-term memory in the hippocampal region of the brain and making it stick. This is done through specific techniques for memorization and rehearsal. Indeed, we regard those who know facts and theories off the tops of their heads as experts. We'll cover this aspect in more detail in a later chapter.

The second way that learning and expertise occur neurologically is through the myelin portion of the neuron, which enables someone to think faster and more intensely. Of course, we also deem people who can solve problems quickly or think creatively as experts.

A brief neuroscience review may be helpful for greater context: neurons are the cellular building blocks of the brain. A neuron is made up of three main components:

- Dendrites - receive signals *from* other neurons
- Cell body - processes those signals
- Axon - sends messages *to* other neurons

The signals that are sent and received are called nerve impulses, which are tiny electrical charges that travel from the dendrite, through the cell body, and out the axon to the next neuron in the brain. It's an incredibly fast process—consider how you might be able to catch something you've dropped before it hits the floor. It's faster than that! This chain of electrical impulses is the physical representation of our thoughts. Yes, this means our thoughts do have an actual upper limit on their speed.

What relates neurons to learning and expertise is myelin, the fatty tissue that covers the majority of the neuron itself. In essence, the more myelin, the faster the electrical signals are. Really, it's all about the myelin.

One compelling set of evidence comes from brain scans of expert musicians—classical pianists. There was shown to be a strong correlation between the amount of myelin in regions that a pianist would ostensibly use—the fine motor skills, visual, and auditory processing parts of the brain. These areas had a far higher amount of myelin as compared to non-musicians.

Another point in favor of myelin's expertise-enhancing abilities is what happens when it is missing. *Demyelination* is a known factor in multiple sclerosis and other neurodegenerative diseases that cause symptoms such as loss of dexterity, blurry vision, loss of bowel control, and general weakness and fatigue. This suggests that myelin is an important factor in allowing us to make the most of our brain.

It may be surprising to hear that there is such a tangible, biological representation of learning and expertise. Talent and competence, then, are not some abstract qualities that are mysteriously granted on some and not others. Instead, it's a manifestation of the brain's ordinary functioning – your brain included!

After all, the brain, for all its complex manifestations and philosophical conceptions, is a physical piece of flesh and blood that gets tired, needs fuel, and doesn't always function at its best. The brain, just like any other piece of physical flesh and blood, has optimal conditions under which it functions, learns, and creates expertise.

As such, we should treat it like any other muscle. The brain consumes glucose and is composed mostly of water. It needs time to recover and has its own limits. When you overwork it, performance drops. When you think about it, it should be obvious that overall bodily health should and will affect your brain's learning abilities. Again, our cultural conception of experts or intelligent people as merely disembodied "brains on legs" is far from the truth.

If there is a runner and she has a race tomorrow, do you think stress, sleep, and exercise will play a role in getting her ready for the race? She would have regularly exercised to be in her best shape possible, she would have reduced her stress and focused on what she needed to do, and she would have slept as much as possible that night so she is fresh and energetic.

Now, take the brain. Will you retain information better after getting only three hours of sleep, or when you have had a full eight hours? What about if you had to work ninety hours one week, versus thirty-five hours another week? Finally, what if you had a long debate with a friend: are you going to feel fresh and ready to consume information? Even if this runner *did* possess some raw, inborn talent for running, she cannot simply turn up to a race exhausted, unprepared and unpracticed… and expect to win. Just like an athlete and her physical body, the brain must be ready for performance, and the factors of stress, sleep, and exercise greatly influence that.

Let's begin our mini-tour of how neurological health and learning ability is directly correlated to improving your brain's functioning. **Stress** is one of the biggest influences on the brain's health. If you want a clear and concrete illustration, you don't have to look further than any veteran or trauma victim suffering from post-traumatic stress disorder (PTSD) and how their lives are negatively affected. They literally lack the ability to function in daily life because they are so tense, and they are likely to snap at any given moment as an outlet for their anxiety and fear.

A plethora of research has found that both chronic and acute stress impact the brain's health and memory systems in hugely negative ways. This is in large part due to the body's physiological response to stress. But first, it will be helpful to define the difference between the two main types of stress: chronic and acute stress.

Chronic stress is when you are under ongoing stress for a relatively long period of time—something as small as being under a constant heavy load at work or dealing with a relationship that is frequently combative. These are the small sources of stresses that seem insignificant until you look at the cumulative effects. When we are experiencing chronic stress (again, the amount of which is highly variable and relative to the person's tolerance), our body is in a state of physiological arousal. This is known as the fight-or-flight response, and it's our body's main defense mechanism when it senses stress or fear.

It was once useful millennia ago when the terms "fight" and "flight" were truly taken literally—if the body sensed a stressor or a reason to be in fear, it would put itself on the highest levels of alertness and be prepared for a fight to the death, if necessary, or running away as quickly as possible. In either case, the body's hormones, heart rate, and blood pressure are highly elevated. The main stress hormone, cortisol, is released in spades to maintain the alertness.

So if you are under chronic stress, you are *permanently* in this fight-or-flight mode and have an excess of cortisol. Except, this mode was not something your body evolved to experience for the long term. Your body will very rarely reach the relaxation phase, which is known as a state of homeostasis. In other words, chronic stress makes you alert and physiologically aroused *all the time*. This is exhausting both physically and mentally, and has the effect of shrinking your brain. Studies have shown that chronic stress has caused as big as a 14 percent decrease in hippocampal volume, which is startling.

The hippocampus is one of the main areas for memory processing and storage in the brain. Another study (Pasquali, 2006) showed that memory in rats was negatively affected when the rats were exposed to cats, which presumably caused stress. The rats that were exposed to cats far more routinely were unable to locate certain entrances and exits. It was both cute and horrifying.

Chronic stress will cause all those negative effects in you, and the difficult part is you may not realize you are under chronic stress, because it has become normalized. It is just like when your shoulders tense up—you probably don't realize it until someone points it out and you can see the contrast between being relaxed and being hypervigilant.

The cumulative effects of being constantly on edge, paranoid, unable to focus, and feeling despair and overwhelm will catch up to you.

Imagine being pumped up on adrenaline for days, weeks, or months. Not only will it impair your memory and brain processing, it will leave you unable to function in general. This is what people with PTSD suffer, but to a much higher degree.

Acute stress, on the other hand, is not something that will slide by unnoticed.

Acute stress is the sudden jolt of adrenaline you experience when someone cuts you off in traffic and you nearly crash, or you get into a heated argument. Incidentally, many opportunities for acute stress tend to occur in traffic situations. It might even involve getting into a car accident. However, acute stress is momentary, temporary, and you can feel it and notice it. Intense bouts of acute stress can cause headaches, muscle tension, upset stomach, or vomiting. This is when adrenaline is coursing through your veins, trying to give you the alertness and strength you need for anything. If it persists and lasts for a longer period of time, it just may cross the threshold into chronic stress.

But the labels aren't our main concern. What's important is what happens to the learning and memory-processing systems when you are under any type of stress.

You can also think of the brain in this state as simply being occupied with thoughts of stress and anxiety, so much so that it is unable to divert brainpower to memory and thinking clearly. This wouldn't be an inaccurate characterization of the role of stress. Stress can literally change your brain's structure and size, so it's something to devote a bit more attention to.

Make sure that the engine of your brain is running right when you need it. Ask yourself what the major sources of anxiety are in your life. They might be people, work, or even material objects. Whatever the case, make sure you are only doing what you need to and nothing unnecessarily on behalf of others.

The next part of the healthy brain equation is sleep. It has long been argued that specific modes of sleep are where memories are actually created, and where learning can be said to occur. It is thought that the brain's structure is changed and synaptic connections are formed during sleep.

Indeed, studies have teased out the specifics of how memories are enhanced or stored during sleep. In a 2005 study, Professor Matthew Walker of Harvard University was able to compare fMRI scans of the brains of subjects while awake and asleep to see the different parts of the brain that were activated—where memory consolidation occurred. He found that people's cerebellums were far more active after a period of sleep between periods of learning, and this activity was highly correlated with better learning and memory.

Professor Walker commented, "Sleep appears to play a key role in human development. At twelve months of age, infants are in an almost constant state of motor skill learning, coordinating their limbs and digits in a variety of routines. They have an immense amount of new material to consolidate, and consequently, this intensive period of learning may demand a great deal of sleep."

Specifically, rapid eye movement (REM) sleep is most important for memory consolidation and storage during sleep. There has been debate in recent years about just how important it is to memory, but sleep can also serve another purpose: we sleep to forget the unimportant facets of our day and filter them out so our memories can be more organized.

In 2003, research conducted at the University of Wisconsin-Madison hypothesized that neurons and synapses essentially worked and proliferated in overload during the day, and were pruned back during sleep so only the important items made it into longer-term memory. This implied that we sleep to literally forget certain parts of our day and to have better-organized minds.

Sleep can serve many specific purposes for the brain and memory, but overall, the brain, like the body, needs rest and recovery. A team of researchers from the University of Rochester have also posited that sleep is like the brain's "waste removal system." When you can provide the systems responsible for memory a reprieve overnight, it is simply likely they will continue to work better for you in the coming days.

The final piece of the puzzle is exercise. It might be surprising to hear that physical exercise is just as good for your brain as it is for your muscles and bones, but it's been proven time and time again.

One particular study was conducted at Radboud University in the Netherlands. Male and female subjects took a memory test, and then one third of them exercised immediately after the test, one third of them exercised four hours after the test, and the remaining third did not exercise after the test. The subjects were collected two days later to repeat the same memory test, and the group who exercised four hours after the initial test performed the best without fail. It appeared that exercise was effective in helping the brain stabilize and store the memory.

Other studies take the physiological angle and point to the neurotransmitters and hormones that exercise releases and how they affect memory processes. Exercise is instrumental in the production of a brain protein called FNDC5, which eventually releases brain-derived neurotrophic factor (BDNF). BDNF has been shown to aid general brain functioning and memory processing by preserving existing brain cells, promoting growth of new brain cells, and encouraging overall brain growth. Human brains tend to shrink when we grow older, but exercise, which creates BDNF, can literally increase the size of your brain.

Your brain primarily uses glucose (what carbohydrates are converted into) for fuel, and when that is not available, it begins to use fat for fuel. It is when the brain starts to use fat for fuel that BDNF creation is triggered. This is possibly behind the science of fasting and why low-carbohydrate diets have been shown to report high amounts of alertness and cognitive acuity as pleasant side effects (Fond, 2012).

Your brain has the highest oxygen requirement of any organ in your body, up to 20 percent of your entire body's usage. When you can exercise and improve your cardiovascular systems and ensure that blood is pumping better through your arteries, you will have greater access to oxygen. It's the same with water—the brain is, on average, 70 percent composed of water, and exercise makes you more aware of hydration.

Exercise does have its limits, however. The best types of exercise are those that increase blood flow and burn fat. If exercise becomes too strenuous and difficult, then you begin to create stress, and you've already read how detrimental stress can be on your mental faculties. Overall, it appears that the maxim of healthy body, healthy mind holds very true.

It's just another case of why we should have listened to our mothers more when we were young.

Sleep as much as possible, exercise often, and don't sweat the small things. When we can avoid the stressors in our life, we can devote more mental bandwidth to that which matters. You wouldn't be great at studying for a test if your dog was missing, would you? We can better comprehend and absorb difficult material when we have a full night's sleep.

Finally, exercise is not only invigorating and important for giving you a mental break, but it can cause chemical changes in the brain that benefit your memory processes. The brain is the engine of learning and expertise, and you have to be mindful of priming it for optimal performance.

Takeaways:

- Expertise can be achieved and thought of in many ways, but one of the big obstacles you may have to overcome is the myth of innate talent and how it relates to the fixed versus growth mindset.

- The myth of innate talent is that only certain people have enough talent to become experts—not true. This can be further supported by noting the differences between the fixed mindset (I can't improve) versus the growth mindset (I can improve). Whatever you put your efforts toward, you can learn and grow expertise in. It's not that you just have to use "the power of belief" or something ephemeral like that, it's just a linear equation requiring effort and time.
- The biology of expertise is surprisingly simple. Think of the brain like a muscle, and it becomes clearer. Learning and expertise take hold largely because of an increase of myelin, a fatty acid that covers neurons and increases the speed and strength of electrical impulses—i.e., thoughts.
- Being flesh and blood, the brain has the same requirements as a bicep or hamstring. This means the presence of stress (both chronic and acute), the quality and amount of sleep, and the frequency of exercise have large effects on just how effectively you can learn.

Chapter 2. How to Find, Intake, and Understand Info Better and Faster

The first step in developing expertise always involves information. You're either searching for it, obtaining it, synthesizing it, or using it. Information is the currency of expertise! Fortunately, we live in times when information is almost ridiculously easy to find, thanks to the Internet. Ask anyone who's spent a day on the internet, though, and they'll tell you that not all information is created equal. This ends up being a double-edged sword, as you'll inevitably need to discern what really matters in your quest for expertise. We need to learn how to learn, and we need to identify those quality sources of information before we actually understand them – a little like pulling yourself up by your intellectual bootstraps!

Instead of devoting your time to learning, the quest sometimes becomes identifying what is important—you have to *find* that information among all the useless data you don't need.

Imagine a detective looking for clues to a crime that happened in the middle of a small town, but using crime data for the entire country to get to the bottom of it. It would be a fruitless pursuit.

This is why it's not enough to just have a wealth of information at your disposal. To be of value, information has to be processed, analyzed, and fully comprehended. You need a framework, a process, and a goal to which all your efforts are dedicated. Just as learning a new skill takes repeated practice, taking in new knowledge requires exercising your mind. The biggest mistake you can make is to assume that the right information will just fall into your lap at the right time!

This chapter will guide you through the practice of gathering and handling information, from knowing absolutely nothing to becoming an educated expert. It's about how to deal with the most valuable resource experts can possess. Not only will you be able to process information more skillfully, you'll also do so more swiftly and efficiently. That's where we start with the first section.

The Research Process from A to Z

The first step in building expertise in anything is research: the step-by-step process of reading and analyzing materials relevant to your chosen field of interest. But before we can understand and synthesize, we must find *what* we will be studying. It's a process that isn't inherently difficult, but many minefields exist that can derail your learning.

There is no shortage of information about almost everything, and we have better access to data and facts than we ever have before. But the sheer amount of information we have can make us forget how to research effectively. Many of us simply equate having information handy with possessing intelligence. If the facts are within immediate reach, we sometimes figure that's all we need. But without *understanding* what the data means or having a good sense of the context, that data is of no value. This is not even mentioning that the facts you have might be biased, skewed, or flat-out inaccurate. Today, the threat is greater than ever of falling into a "filter bubble" where information is skewed, distorted or flat-out incorrect. How can we steer clear of questionable sources and make sure our research will bear fruit?

Today, something like tertiary education is being demoted in the public imagination because of the wealth of free textbooks, original sources, videos and lectures available for free. Though it's true that this material may be the same that someone else pays for, there is also value in being exposed to certain curated materials at a certain point in the process, as well as having a mentor who can stand outside our learning and prompt, correct and guide it. When we do research on our own, we have to perform this role for ourselves. We have to take care about our learning, how it will progress, and what standards it will follow.

Research is a gradual process. It's methodical and investigative – it's also iterative and self-corrects continuously. More than just accumulating data and statistics, the successful research project makes one feel comfortable and assured in explaining the full story behind the topic one chooses. And even though it's systematic and can require patience, a solid research plan can help you build expertise much more quickly than you might think.

These five steps of research, if executed thoughtfully and correctly, will give you what you need to gain mental command over a new topic. It's important to hit all five steps without skipping any. You'll be able to understand a concept, issue, or problem from a variety of angles and approaches. Not only will this give you theoretical insight, but you'll also feel more confident in your own abilities. Nothing shatters a stubborn fixed mindset like evidence that you are actually learning something and improving!

These steps are somewhat similar to the well-known scientific method (create hypothesis, question, collect data, test hypothesis, analyze, and conclude). Both methods call for mindful adherence to each step in the process. Whereas the scientific method is used to test theories based on pre-existing knowledge, the research method is a way to obtain entirely new knowledge or insight. Research is what allows people to generate theories to later test. One seeks to answer a narrow question, the other seeks to explore a wide and possibly undefined space. They are both systematic processes for learning about a desired topic.

We'll go through a thorough example after describing these steps to illustrate just what each item entails.

1. Gather information. The first step is to retrieve as much data about a topic as you possibly can. Collect anything and everything from as wide a range of sources as you can manage.

At this early stage of research, don't be too discriminating. Get as much as you can from wherever you can find it. Think what it would be like if you searched on Google about a certain topic, got ten pages or more of results, and clicked on every single link. The point isn't to get immediate answers; it's to get an initial, panoramic overview of the subject you're investigating.

So, don't be too restrictive—open the floodgates. Organize the information you gather into general topics, arguments, and opinions. Get a "feel" for the major themes you keep encountering. You might find that you are more confused after this stage than when you started—that's fine and natural. What's important is that you have everything in front of you, from shallow to deep, and from correct to dubious. At this stage, you don't make any judgments about what you're uncovering.

2. Filter your sources. Now that you've got all the information you need, it's time to identify what your sources are, what kind of information they present, and whether it's good or not. This step could reduce the amount of information you'll study by 75 percent or even more.

Every information outlet has a different intent and approach to the subject matter it discusses. Some concentrate on hard and straight data. Some offer narrative accounts or anecdotes relating to the subject, while others provide editorial opinions or theories. Some sources are official agencies or authorities in your chosen field, while others are trade papers, media, groups, or associations who are interested in it. Some are simply blogs of opinionated people who have taken an interest in a particular topic with no expertise or common sense. And yes, some are "fake news."

Your goal here is to draw out the good sources and disregard the bad ones. A good source backs up its arguments and ideas with solid data, confirmable truth, and careful examination. A bad source is generally more interested in persuading through emotions and hyperbole and might rely on misleading or utterly wrong data to do so. A bad source may have an agenda – that isn't your neutral education!

Don't confuse anecdote with evidence, even if there are multiple anecdotes. After all, that's how every single old wives' tale was started. Anecdote is important, but is not a replacement for objective fact.

Good sources are also, generally, well-established with a solid track record in accuracy; bad sources are often fly-by-night operations that have no published credibility. A legitimate source is also likely to have an actual real name connected to it. With a few notable exceptions (like Deep Throat in the Watergate scandal), anonymous or cloaked identities are usually sketchy as authentic leads. Also consider how your sources are regarded by other sources, or if they are shunned or altogether ignored. Look closely at this shunning itself – without going down any conspiracy rabbit holes, who is most vocal, and how do they benefit by promoting their narrative version of events? Who benefits when certain speakers, voices, or opinions are hidden?

At this stage, you'll start noticing some divisions in the research you've collected. You'll see certain sources' tendencies and inclinations. You'll get a sense of which are the most popular or common outlooks (the majority), which are the rarer or more unusual viewpoints (the minority), and which ones are straight-up crazy ramblings from the minds of lunatics (the crackpots). In today's world, knowing how to draw these lines is not easy, and yesterday's crackpots are frequently today's truthtellers.One way around these minefields is to tune into your own objectives and goals in learning. You'll be able to divide up the sources and retain the ones that are most reliable and helpful.

3. Look for Patterns and Overlap. As you're viewing and reviewing all your source material, you'll begin to notice recurring topics, stances, and ideas. Certain points will crop up more frequently, and some will only appear once, seemingly randomly. You'll see certain ideas reappear, but slightly changed according to the source. You'll start getting a better idea of the primary points, secondary points, and boundaries of the subject you're looking into. You'll get a feel for what is not said, not known or not considered relevant. You'll also be able to build bridges between parallel ideas and points of overlap.

Here you'll be able to identify the major components of your topic, and the most prevalent thoughts and beliefs. Generally, the best sources will talk about the same things, so when that happens, you can safely assume they're the most important parts of your subject. You can see where the main points bump into each other, where they end, and where they rarely go. In this way, you can truly get a sense of the landscape and the different opinions and voices that exist to inform your own expertise.

When you see a point repeated by multiple sources, it's a good sign that you should consider it a major idea or theme. Likewise, if a detail is rarely mentioned by notable people in the field, or it doesn't fit into the prevalent views, you know it's probably not something that moves the needle, or is too new to be considered valuable.

This isn't to say less common or alternate points of view are necessarily wrong—they aren't. But use your better judgment. If only one isolated source is making a certain assertion, even if they have "disciples" who agree with all they say, there's a much higher chance that they're discussing something that's not really true, or at least not very important. It would be wrong to focus on this point of view at the expense of others, and generate a view on the topic that doesn't reflect the reality on the ground. Separate things on which you need to focus from elements that will ultimately bog down your work.

You should understand what the main points and arguments are (and why), as well as a few of the minor ones, by the end of this step. Getting through this stage alone may qualify you as an expert relative to others, and it's common that most people stop their journey and education here. But if you stop here, you risk falling prey to *confirmation bias* and not knowing what you don't know.

4. Seek dissenting opinions. By this point, you'll no doubt have a theory or opinion in mind. You'll also have whittled down your sources to support that. If you're like most people, your unspoken bias has led you specifically to seek out information that already accords with foregone conclusions you have. So, now's the time to look for sources that disagree with you. This is a hugely important step. Without knowing the full extent of opposing arguments, you won't have the complete picture that you need to understand the issue. No matter how convinced you are, try to find one.

Don't be afraid to question your own viewpoints by playing devil's advocate. If there's a minor quibble you have about your theory, this is the point where you indulge your imagination. Instead of rushing in to defend it and explain away these niggles, get curious about them. Imagine all possible scenarios and circumstances where your theory might be put to the test. After all, almost no theory has a 100 percent approval rate, even if it seems like there is a scientific consensus. Even if this mythical theory were to exist, this is an exercise in gaining perspective and nuanced expertise, not necessarily in right or wrong.

Finding dissenting opinions is an important step in avoiding the all-too-common plague of confirmation bias—our human tendency to hear and see only what we want to hear and see. This is when someone dearly wants for a certain thing to be true, so they reject any solid evidence that it's false and only accept information that confirms their beliefs. That leads them to cherry-pick data that supports their point and ignore hard proof that disproves it. Confirmation bias is not objective, so it has no place in actual research. It's worse when bias is unconscious, because we cannot take steps to remove a bias we don't think we have. To combat this tendency, give the voice of the opposition clear and full attention.

You don't have to abandon your ideas entirely, but being realistic about criticisms against it actually give you the opportunity to arrive at a stronger, more useful position. One of the prerequisites for learning is to humbly and honestly acknowledge what is not currently understood. So, get into the habit of admitting when you don't know, or when your own personal inclinations are getting in the way.

At this point, you may arrive at a conclusion that's been put through the paces. You have sophistication and nuance. The point is legitimate and not clouded by fallacies, misunderstanding, or disinformation. You'll comprehend your own beliefs more fully and understand why others may have different ideas. You'll be able to articulate precisely why you believe what you believe. And you will have the strength to continually adjust and adapt what you believe!

You may come across opinions or assumptions with which you strongly disagree. You might be tempted to discount these alternate perspectives. But you need to absorb them as fully as you can, no matter how false or mistaken you believe them to be. There's a reason these other opinions exist, and only by understanding them from an objective standpoint will you gain a complete view of the subject's landscape.

5. Put it all together. This is the point where you make your statement—only after you've considered all the above, rather than "shooting first and asking questions later." This is a point of clarity for you. You can explain all aspects of the topic or issue you're talking about. Write, speak, outline, or mind-map confidently about your new area of knowledge. Here's an easy way to think about how you summarize your expertise: put everything together to show how you understand the whole situation, including the small and nuanced points: "X, Y, and Z because . . . *however* A, B, and C because . . ." If you can't do this with certainty, you may need to go back a step or two in the process.

Let's explore an example that illustrates all these steps at work, and with at least a clear path for anyone who wishes to be an expert on a certain topic. For the sake of description, let's say you have a deep and driving need to become an expert in the *protest movements of the 1960s*.

Gather your info. Accumulate all the information you can without discrimination: history books, news articles, biographies, blogs, History Channel videos, websites, Congressional minutes, newsreels—anything. You're just herding in all the info you can in this stage. Any information is good information at this point. Use all mediums at your disposal. Don't forget to start your organization immediately by grouping and categorizing thoughts and opinions.

Filter your sources. Do you have news clippings from established sources like the *New York Times* or *Time* magazine? Are the stories verifiable? Do your biographies and nonfiction books provide meaningful information that's backed up, or are they thought pieces that don't rely on much data at all? Are the blogs you're looking at dependably referenced, or are they sloppily put together and filled with hyperbole? Are you actually just watching *Drunk History?* This point is where you use your discrimination and decide what sources are worth listening to (even if they have rare arguments) and which ones you should ditch (even if they parrot popular stances). Sorry to say it, but some opinions are worth more than others.

Look for patterns. Examine your sources for repeated mentions or descriptions of similar events—say, the Civil Rights Act, the assassination of JFK, the 1968 Democratic Convention. Look for similar trends across varied eras: economic status, unemployment rates, election results, specific gatherings or protests. The more often a certain event or trend appears in your review, the more likely it is to have been truly impactful on the subject. Examine all the views you can find: majority opinion, minority opinion, and even the crackpot ideas. Uncovering repeated patterns will give you a more three-dimensional view of the landscape.

Seek dissenting opinions. Hopefully by now you've formed a working thesis; now you put it to the test by finding well-reasoned opposing viewpoints. Ideally, some of your filtered reading material contains at least one counterargument that has rationally constructed viewpoints. Alternately, doing a (very careful) Google search might produce some results. Weigh these dissenting opinions against your argument and consider where you may need to adjust certain parts of your contentions. Assume that everyone believes wholeheartedly that they are correct, and you will be more open to seeking people's stances instead of shutting them down.

Dig into not only what that opinion is, but why it is held and the assumptions it is based on. Insert whatever conspiracy theory you may have heard through the grapevine about prominent assassinations, and you'll get the idea—why do those ideas exist and who do they benefit?

Put it all together. Whether you keep it private or publish it, summarize your discoveries and opinions and keep them closely available. Make sure you've accounted for as many viewpoints as you can from both supportive and opposing viewpoints. For example, you may feel that protest movements of the '60s arose from sincere desire for change, but may have come across some opinions that said they were inside jobs coordinated by the government. Leave room for the dissenting conclusions of others—they'll give your final result more body and legitimacy. Remember "X, Y, and Z because . . . *however* A, B, and C because . . ."

Next-Level Reading and Consumption

Let's backtrack to the first part of the research when you've accumulated the information you need. Especially if you've gathered a considerable amount of reading material, you'll want to find a way to understand it as fully as possible. The prospect can be daunting. Perhaps the reading material is complex or exhaustive or can't be consumed in one chunk. How do you take in the information you need and really read to effectively increase your knowledge? There are two frameworks we can use to truly absorb and make the most of a resource, and there is some overlap between them.

The first is generally deemed the *four levels of reading*, and they were developed by philosopher Mortimer Adler in his suitably titled publication *How to Read a Book*. Adler explains that reading is not a single, universally consistent act. He breaks up the act of reading into four individual levels that differ in purpose, effort, and the amount of time they take. Furthermore, different tiers apply to different kinds of reading—some books can be appropriate for all levels, while others just support one or two. Especially in the higher two levels, faithfully following these tiers of reading will greatly advance your expertise on the subject.

Adler's four levels of reading, from simplest to most complex, are:

- Elementary
- Inspectional
- Analytical
- Syntopical

Elementary. You're already past this level. This is, essentially, learning to read. It's the kind of reading that's taught in elementary school. You're learning what the letters are, how words are pronounced, and what they objectively mean. It's knowing that the sentence "The cat is on the bed" means there's a cat on the bed, and that it *doesn't* say there's a dog on the couch. Blows the mind, right?

The elementary stage also applies to an adult who's learning a new language and has to be trained to understand new alphabets, vocabulary, and pronunciation. It also describes a student reading a technical textbook for the first time who has to learn new syntax or specific jargon. Anytime you come upon a new language, dialect, or lexicon, you're doing elementary reading.

Inspectional. The next level up for readers is understanding the essence of a certain book—but not digesting the whole of it. It's called the inspectional stage, and it's sometimes disparaged or discounted by avid readers. But in developing expertise, it's a very valuable process.

Inspectional reading actually has two mini-stages of its own:

- *Systematic skimming.* This is casually examining certain elements of a book apart from the body of the text: skimming the table of contents and the index, or reading the preface or the blurb on the back inside jacket. If you're assessing an e-book, it could mean reading the online description and customer reviews as well. Systematic skimming gives you enough information to know what the book is and how you would classify it: "it's a novel about World War II," or "it's a book that explains how to cook French cuisine." That's it.

- *Superficial reading.* This stage is actually reading the book but in a very casual way. You start at the beginning and take in the material without consuming it or thinking too much about it. You don't make notes in the margins. You don't look up unfamiliar phrases or concepts—if there's a passage you don't understand, you just proceed to the next part. In superficial reading, you're getting a sense of the tone, rhythm, and general direction of the book, rather than absorbing every single element of the narrative.

Inspectional reading is something like a recon mission or a survey. You're just getting a sense of what the book is about and the reading experience. You might pick up on a couple of very broad, general ideas in the book, but you won't go very deeply into them. You'll just find out what you might be in for, and then you'll decide whether you're interested enough to go more in-depth.

For example, let's say you're looking at a book on classical music. In your systematic skimming, you'd see the title and subtitle. You'd read the back flap, which says it's "an in-depth but gently irreverent study of classical composers." You'd read the table of contents—there are chapters entitled "Wagner in Drag," "Mozart's Cat

Imitations," and "Beethoven's Love of Rats." At this point, you've probably ascertained that this is *not* a terribly serious work and not one that's likely to add to your expertise, although it may be entertaining.

Why should a budding expert go through this stage and not just skip to the next level? Even though it's not a deep dive, it gives you a lot of answers. You'll get a sense of the writer's approach: is it serious, comical, or satirical? Does it rely on real-life accounts or imaginary situations? Is it heavy on statistics? Does it quote a lot of outside sources? Are there pictures?

Having a good sense of the answers to those questions will help you frame the content and define your expectations, which—if you've decided to proceed with the book—will make the next level of reading more productive.

Analytical. The third level of reading is the deepest level for consuming a single book or volume of work—it's full digestion of, *and interaction with*, the material at hand. The challenge of analytical reading is simply: "If time were not an object, how thoroughly would you read this book?"

Analytical reading can be described as taking the book out of the author's hands and making it your own. You don't just read the text; you highlight or underline key points, and you make commentary or ask questions. In a way, you can use the marginalia to simulate an ongoing conversation with the writer.

The goal of analytical reading is to understand the material well enough so you can explain it to someone else without a lot of effort. You're able to describe the subject very concisely. You're able to list its parts in order and say how they connect with each other. You're able to understand and specify the issues the writer's concerned with and what problems they're trying to resolve.

For example, if you're reading Stephen Hawking's *A Brief History of Time*, you'd highlight key phrases in the first part about the history of physics: the Big Bang theory, black holes, and time travel, for example. You might asterisk the names of Copernicus and Galileo with a note to research them more fully. You might question Hawking's explanation of the expanding universe with writing in the margins.

Analytical reading is hard work. But it's the level at which the thrill of gaining new understanding is most profound and rewarding. This kind of interaction with reading makes learning proactive—instead of just listening to what some person's telling you, it's more like you're extracting the information yourself. When you're doing that, you're engaging more of your mind, and that means it's far more likely you're going to *remember* what you've learned. That's a much easier path toward expertise.

Syntopical. In the final level of reading, you work with multiple books or pieces of material covering the same subject. One could describe syntopical reading as "compare/contrast," but it's actually a lot deeper than that. (And syntopical reading is not to be confused with the similarly spelled *synoptical* reading, which is pretty much its exact opposite.)

At this stage, you're trying to understand the entire breadth of the subject you're studying, not just a single volume about it. Sound familiar? You analyze the differences in the ideas, syntax, and arguments presented in the books and compare them. You're able to identify and fill any gaps in knowledge you might have. You're conversing with multiple partners, forming and arranging the most pressing questions you need to answer. You're identifying all the issues and aspects of the subjects that the books cover and looking up phraseology and vocabulary that you don't understand.

Syntopical reading is a relatively major commitment, almost like a semester-long college course you're teaching yourself. Think of it as an active effort, something one doesn't normally associate with the relaxing act of reading a novel.

It's like a TV show or movie in which someone's trying to unravel a multilayered criminal enterprise. Somewhere in the movie, they show a giant bulletin board in the station with drawings, Post-its, and pictures of people, with pieces of yarn showing how they're all interconnected. When new information is discovered from different sources, it all gets added to that board. That's what syntopical reading is like: it's a concerted effort to find the answers and increase your expertise, and you don't even have to deal with the mob. You can concentrate on more lawful subjects like Occam's razor, absurdist theater, or the stock market.

These four levels serve as connected steps that gradually make a subject approachable, more relevant, and finally, fully familiar to you.

In the elementary stage—well, you're learning to read. You kind of need that for everything.

In the inspectional phase, you're getting an overview of the framework and structure and gauging your interest. You're priming yourself in case you decide to commit to the analytical phase by estimating what's in store for you at a deeper level.

In the analytical phase, you're committing to an extensive effort to understand as much of the subject as you can from as many viewpoints as possible. You're absorbing and questioning the book, and creating further curiosity about the topic it addresses, driving yourself to learn more.

In the syntopical phase, you've "graduated," in a sense, from a single or limited perspective of the subject to a holistic study of all its elements. This is where you're layering the levels of your expertise at multiple points—something you can't even comprehend in typically casual or recreational reading.

Another framework for getting the most out of a resource is called the SQ3R method, developed by American educator Francis P. Robinson. It is named for its five components:

- survey
- question
- read
- recite
- review

Survey. The first step in the method is getting a general overview of what you'll be reading. Textbooks and nonfiction works aren't like fiction or narrative literature in which you just start from the beginning and wind your way through each chapter. The best works of nonfiction are arranged to impart information in a way that's clear and memorable and builds upon each previous chapter. If you dive in without surveying first, you are going in blind, without understanding where you are going and what you are trying to accomplish. You should get a lay of the land first, *before* you delve into Chapter 1. The survey component enables you to get the most general introduction to the topic so you can establish and shape the goals you want to achieve from reading the book.

It's just like taking a look at the entire map before you set off on a road trip. You may not need all the knowledge at the moment, but understanding everything as a whole and how it fits together will help you with the small details and when you're in the weeds. You'll know that you generally need to head southwest if you're confused.

In the SQ3R method, surveying means examining the structure of the work: the book title, the introduction or preface, section titles, chapter titles, headings and subheadings. If the book is illustrated with pictures or graphics, you'd review them. You could also make note of the conventions the book uses to guide your reading: typefaces, bold or italic text, and chapter objectives and study questions if they're in there. In using the survey step, you're setting up expectations for what you're going to be reading about and giving yourself an initial framework to structure your goals for reading the material.

Beyond books, you should survey all the important concepts in a discipline. If you can't find it within a structure like a book's table of contents, then you need to be able to create it for yourself. Yes, this is the difficult part, but once you are able to lay all the concepts out and understand how they relate to each other at least on a surface level, you will already be leaps ahead of others. Use the survey component to form an outline of what you'll learn. In a sense, it's more like you're plotting out a metaphorical "book" for yourself.

In this phase, you'll want to determine exactly what you *want* to become knowledgeable about, as specifically as you can make it. For example, if you want to learn all about psychology, that's going to take a significant amount of time. It won't happen in one shot. You'd want to specify it a little more: the early history of psychoanalysis, the works of Sigmund Freud and Carl Jung, sports psychology, developmental psychology—the possibilities are plentiful.

You'll want to keep an eye out for phrases or concepts that appear in several different sources, since they represent elements that come up often in your chosen field and might be things you have to know. Draw connections and cause-and-effect relationships before even diving into any of the concepts in detail.

Question. In the second stage of the SQ3R method, you're still not diving into the deep end. During the question stage, you'll work a little more deeply to prepare your mind to focus and interact with the material you're reading. You'll take a slightly closer look at the structure of the book and form some questions you want answered or set up the objectives you hope to achieve.

In the question phase of reading a book—or, more precisely at this point, *preparing* to read—you'd go through the chapter titles, headings, and subheadings and rephrase them in the form of a question. This turns the dry title the author has given into a challenge or problem for you to solve. For example, if you're reading a book on Freud, there might be a chapter called "Foundations of Freud's Analyses of Dreams." You'd rewrite this chapter title as "How did Sigmund Freud's work on dream interpretation originate, and what were his very first ideas on the subject?" You could pencil that question in the margin of your book. If you're reading a textbook with study questions at the ends of the chapters, those serve as excellent guides to what you're about to find out.

Now that you've organized your resources for study planning, you can arrange some of the topics you're going to cover into questions you want answered or objectives you want to meet. Based on the source material you've lined up and the patterns you might have observed, what specific answers are you hoping to find in your studies? Write them down. This is also a good time to come up with a structure for answering your questions—a daily journal, a self-administered quiz, some kind of "knowledge tracker"? You don't have to answer the questions yet—you just need to know how you're going to record them when you do.

Reading. In this stage you're finally ready to dive into the material. Because you've gotten the lay of the land and formed some questions and goals for your studies, you're a little more engaged when you finally sit down to read. You're looking for answers to the questions you've raised. Another underrated aspect of formulating and organizing before you actually begin reading is to build *anticipation* for learning. You've been looking over everything for a while now, and you'll probably be eager to finally dive in and answer the questions you've been mentally accumulating.

This step is where most people try to start but fail because they lack a foundation and instead have unreasonable expectations.

Now you're being deliberate and paced about your reading so you can comprehend better. This means slowing down—a *lot.* Be patient with the material and with yourself. If a passage is difficult to understand, read it extremely slowly. If you aren't getting clarity about a certain part, stop, go back to the beginning, and reread it. It's not like you're reading a page-turner novel that you can't put down. You're reading information that might be densely packed—so tackle it slowly and attentively, one section at a time.

Chances are that reading is part of your study plan, but so might visual aids, online courses, and Internet resources be. Use them exactly the way you'd use the book in the reading phase:

deliberately and persistently, with the goal of fully understanding each concept you're being taught. If you get lost, remember the rewind button and scrolling are your best buddies. Plan your study time around getting as complete a level of comprehensiveness as you can.

Reciting. This step is crucial in processing the information you're learning about and is the biggest difference between reading to learn and reading for entertainment. Now that you're familiar with the material, the aim of the reciting phase is to reorient your mind and attention to focus and learn more fully as you go along. In other words, this step is about literal recitation.

Ask questions—out loud, verbally—about what you're reading. This is also the point where you take copious notes in the margins of the text and underline or highlight key points. Recitation occurs verbally and also through writing. However, it's important to restate these points *in your own words* rather than just copy phrases from the book onto a piece of paper. By doing this, you're taking the new knowledge and putting it into phrases you already know the meaning of. This makes the information easier to grasp in a language you understand. It makes it significant and meaningful to you.

If you have a geology book, you might rephrase and rewrite key points in the following way, starting from the original text:

> "This comparison suggests that the slow progress of erosion on hills and mountains is similar to the much more rapid and observable changes seen in miniature all about us."

You could rewrite the above into something like this:

> "Mountains and hills experience the same decay as happens in lowlands and rivers, just more slowly. Similar to baseball players."

What I'm doing here is putting one single bit of information into two distinct phrases, one of which I had to come up with myself. This is a huge tool that's used in memorization, and it's also a great way to make the information more meaningful to me personally. I also added a bit about baseball because I like baseball, and it makes the concept instantly understandable when I look back at it. Repeated throughout the course of a whole book, this process multiplies your learning capacity by itself.

The recitation phase in organizing your studies is great because it works across different mediums, and there are plenty of ways you can express your questions and restatements.

Review. The final stage of the SQ3R plan is when you go back over the material that you've studied, refamiliarize yourself with the most important points, and build your skills at memorizing the material.

Robinson breaks this stage down into specific days of the week, but we'll just mention some of the tactics in general. They include writing more questions about important parts you have highlighted, orally answering some of the questions if you can, reviewing your notes, creating flashcards for important concepts and terminology, rewriting the table of contents using your own words, and building out a mind map. Any kind of practice that helps you drill down, take in, and commit information to memory is fair game (though flashcards are especially effective).

This step is meant to strengthen your memory of the material, but it does more than that. It can help you see connections and similarities between different aspects that you might not have picked up at first and put concepts and ideas into greater context. It can also improve your mental organization skills so you can use this practice for other topics.

Think of this step as the natural continuation of the survey. At this point, you've gained an outline of the field, you've gotten into the nitty-gritty, and now you should take a step back, reevaluate, and make updated, more accurate, and insightful connections. Pair that with memorization, and your path to self-learning and expertise becomes essentially a shortcut. Flashcards. Mind maps.

Timelines. Unanswered follow-up questions. Categorizing. Critical analysis, drawing conclusions, and asking, "If X, then what follows or precedes it?"

The SQ3R method is no joke. It's exhaustive and detailed and will take patience and sharp organization to pull off. But if you give yourself the patience and devotion to take each step seriously and slowly, you'll find it incredibly helpful to tackle a complex subject. And each time you do it, it's a little easier than the last.

In explaining the SQ3R method, we briefly skimmed the role of organization and notes and how they impact self-learning. After all, you can't organize everything in your head only and hope to be effective.

Some of the processes in this chapter might seem daunting or impossible at first glance. But remember this: at some point in every expert's life, they knew *nothing* about what they've become experts about. Whether they learned in educational institutions or on their own, they went through a period when they had to gather information in a vacuum and take a deep dive in unfamiliar waters. You are absolutely capable of doing exactly what these experts had to do. In fact, you may have it a little easier than they did and can find your path to expertise simpler to follow than you thought.

Takeaways:

- Expertise is built on information. That's an understatement! Gathering, understanding, and using information is what allows you to brand yourself as an expert; without it, you are just an imposter. This chapter is focused on how to effectively gather information and analyze it for deeper meaning. First, you build your inventory, and then you learn how to use everything you've got.

- This largely comes in the form of the five steps of effective research, and the different types of reading as put forth by Mortimer Adler (as well as the related SQ3R method).

- Effective research is composed of: gathering without discrimination, analyzing your sources, searching for patterns, finding the dissenting opinions, and putting it all together. This allows you to gain sophistication and nuance as opposed to shallow opinions built on anecdotes. Most of us only get halfway through the third step.

- Effective reading comes through understanding the four types of reading and how to make it through all four types to gain expertise. The four types are: elementary, inspectional, analytical, and syntopical. Again, most of us only get halfway through the third step.

- Finally, the SQ3R method for extracting information from a resource. Use it. It stands for survey, question, read, recite, review. This is not just a process for attacking a book, but rather a plan for tackling entire disciplines and fields—and whatever you are trying to learn for yourself. Most people will use some elements of the SQ3R method, such as the read and review portion, but without the other elements, deeper comprehension is rarer and more difficult.

Chapter 3. Unlimited Memory

This is the chapter that some of you might have bought this book for. Memory is one of the most important parts of learning, because that's what we want most of the time—to memorize a lot of information so we can use it for some sort of test or evaluation.

Even though modern society is electronically connected to information like never before, having a good memory is still vital to anybody looking to build their expertise. Superior memory is a common trait that most established experts possess. Recalling important facts, narratives, and data helps your ability to learn *new* information: you don't have to stop midstream and look up details you've forgotten.

Memory is a skill in which some are better than others—there are even memory competitions across the world. But again, following the growth mindset, it doesn't mean that we cannot boost our memory deliberately. There are proven methods and practices that can dramatically help you improve your ability to accurately store and retrieve all the useful information you encounter in the research phase.

All learning takes place in the brain, and it involves real changes to our brain's physical structure. If memory is a storage system that exists within specific neural pathways, then learning is about changing neural pathways to adapt one's behavior and thinking to the emergence of new information. How well you remember comes down to how well you are using this neural machinery. Memory and learning depend on each other because the goal of learning is to assimilate new knowledge into memory, and memory is useless without the ability to learn more.

Thus, it is time to devote a lesson to how to memorize more effectively and retain more information that you may only have seen once. People will wonder how you're doing it because it will seem like you have a superpower. All you're doing is understanding how memory works and taking advantage of it.

First, let's take a quick tour of your memory to see how it works and stores information. That way, everything we are doing can make sense in the grand scheme of our brains.

How Memory Works

Memorization is how we store and retrieve information for use—when you think about it, that's really what learning is, and there are three steps to creating a memory. An error in any of these steps will result in knowledge that is not effectively converted to memory—a weak memory, which is something like the feeling of "I can't remember his name, but he was wearing purple . . ." Have you ever felt like you "knew" something but couldn't explain to others where you had found this information, whose idea it was or what else it connected to? That's a sign that the 3 step memory process wasn't as complete as it could be.

The three steps to a memory are:

1. Encoding
2. Storage
3. Retrieval

Encoding is the step of processing information through your senses. You need to convert the squiggly symbols on the page in front of you into electrochemical signals and structures in your brain, deciding what they mean, what they connect to and how you'll recall them later. We do this constantly, and you are doing it right now. We encode information both consciously and subconsciously through all our senses. If you are reading a book, you are using your eyes to encode information.

How much focus and attention you devote also determines how strong the memory is and, consequently, whether that memory only makes it to your short-term memory or if it passes through the gate to your long-term memory. If you are reading a book while watching television, your encoding is probably not too deep or strong. Many people who think they have bad memories actually don't – they have poor attention, and never correctly stored the memory in the first place.

Storage is the next step after you've experienced information with your senses and encoded it. What happens to the information once it passes through your eyes or ears? There are three choices for where this information can go, and they determine whether it's a memory that you will consciously know exists. There are essentially three memory systems: sensory memory, short-term memory, and long-term memory. Obviously our goals with learning and memory are to store information in long-term memory as opposed to the other types.

The last step of the memory process is **retrieval**, which is when we actually use our memories and can be said to have learned something. You might be able to recall it from nothing, or you might need a cue to bring the memory up. Think of this as a kind of tagging, filing or labeling of memories so they can be searched for in the great database of your mind. Some memories might only be memorized in a sequence or as part of a whole, like reciting the ABCs and then realizing you need to sing it through to remember where one particular letter goes. Usually, however much attention you devote to the storage and encoding phases of memory determines just how easy it is to retrieve those memories.

Accelerating your learning, in a sense, is the same as improving your memory capacity and how absorbent your memory is—the more sponge-like, the better. To do this, you need to improve on every level of memory: encoding, storage, and retrieval. Those are the stages we must practice, and you'll learn strategies to do so in this chapter.

Learning is both the process of improving memory while also getting better at *not forgetting*. Why do we forget? Why can't we remember this fact? How did we ever let something slip from our brains?

Forgetting is usually a failure or shortcoming in the storage process—the information you want only makes it to short-term memory, not long-term. The problem isn't that you can't find the information in your brain; it's that the information wasn't embedded strongly enough to begin with.

Sometimes it's easier to think about forgetting as a failure in learning. There are generally three different ways you retrieve or access your memories:

1. Recall
2. Recognition
3. Relearning

Recall is when you remember a memory without external cues. It's when you can recite something on command in a vacuum—for example, looking at a blank piece of paper and then writing down the capitals of all the countries of the world. When you can recall something, you have the strongest memory of it. You have either rehearsed it enough or attached enough significance to it so that it is an incredibly strong item within your long-term memory.

Recognition is when you can conjure up your memory in the presence of an external cue. It's when you might not be able to remember something by pure recall, but if you get a small clue or reminder, you will be able to remember it.

For example, you may not be able to remember all the capitals of the world, but if you got a clue, such as the first letter of the capital or something that rhymes with the capital, it would be fairly easy to state it.

Relearning is undoubtedly the weakest form of recall. It occurs when you are relearning or reviewing information, and it takes you less effort each subsequent time. For example, if you read a list of country capitals on Monday and it takes you thirty minutes, it should take you fifteen minutes the next day, and so on.

Unfortunately, this is where we mostly lie on a daily basis. We might be familiar with a concept, but we haven't committed enough of it to memory to avoid essentially relearning it when we look at it again. This is what happens when we are new to a topic or we've forgotten most of it already. When you're in the relearning stage, you essentially haven't taken anything past the barrier of short-term memory into long-term memory.

As you can see, forgetting isn't as simple as having something on the tip of your tongue or rummaging through the stores of your brain. There are very specific processes that make it a near-miracle that we actually retain as much as we do. The rest of this lesson is dedicated to ways of defeating forgetting and making information stick in your brain.

In this chapter, we have many techniques to go through, all extremely actionable and immediately usable—these are all ways to improve information absorption and turn your brain into a sponge.

Spaced Repetition

The first method is directly aimed at dealing with beating forgetting. Spaced repetition—otherwise known as distributed practice—is just what it sounds like. With this method, you practice what matters most – retrieving information, again and again.

The reason it is such an important technique in improving your memory is that it battles forgetting directly and allows you to work within the bounds of your brain's capabilities. Other techniques, no less important, are about increasing encoding or storage—remember the three parts of memory are encoding, storage, and retrieval. Spaced repetition helps the last part, retrieval.

Consider someone who spends hours studying for an exam by reading and making notes. Another person spends those same hours doing practice papers. In the exam, the first person flounders – because the exam is the first time they're having to remember all they've encoded. The second person (who practiced spaced repetition) finds it easy, because retrieving stored memories is exactly what they've been practicing.

In order to commit more to memory and retain information better, practice retrieving and not encoding, and space out your rehearsal and exposure to it over as long of a period as possible. In other words, you will remember something far better if you study it for one hour a day versus twenty hours in one weekend. This goes for just about everything you could possibly learn. Additional research has shown that seeing something twenty times in one day is far less effective than seeing something ten times over the course of seven days.

Spaced repetition makes more sense if you imagine your brain as a muscle. Muscles can't be exercised all the time and then put back to work with little-to-no recovery. Your brain needs time to make connections between concepts, create muscle memory, and generally become familiar with something. Sleep has been shown to be where neural connections are made, and it's not just mental. Synaptic connections are formed in your brain, and dendrites are stimulated.

If an athlete works out too hard in one session like you might be tempted to in studying, one of two things will happen. The athlete will either be too exhausted, and the latter half of the workout will be useless, or the athlete will become injured. Rest and recovery are necessary to the task of learning, and sometimes effort isn't what's required.

Here's a look at what a schedule focused on spaced repetition might look like.

Monday at 10:00 a.m. Learn initial facts about Spanish history. You accumulate five pages of notes.

Monday at 8:00 p.m. Review notes about Spanish history, but don't just review passively. Make sure to try to recall the information from your own memory. Recalling is a much better way to process information than simply rereading and reviewing. This might only take twenty minutes.

Tuesday at 10:00 a.m. Try to recall the information without looking at your notes much. After you first try to actively recall as much as possible, go back through your notes to see what you missed, and make note of what you need to pay closer attention to. This will probably take only fifteen minutes.

Tuesday at 8:00 p.m. Review notes. This will take ten minutes.

Wednesday at 4:00 p.m. Try to independently recall the information again, and only look at your notes once you are done to see what else you have missed. This will take only ten minutes. Make sure not to skip any steps.

Thursday at 6:00 p.m. Review notes. This will take ten minutes.

Friday at 10:00 a.m. Active recall session. This will take ten minutes.

Looking at this schedule, note that you are only studying an additional seventy-five minutes throughout the week, but that you've managed to go through the entire lesson a whopping six additional times. Not only that, you've likely committed most of it to memory because you are using active recall instead of passively reviewing your notes.

You're ready for a test the next Monday. Actually, you're ready for a test by Friday afternoon. Spaced repetition gives your brain time to process concepts and make its own connections and leaps because of the repetition.

Think about what happens when you have repeated exposure to a concept. For the first couple of exposures, you may not see anything new. As you get more familiar with it and stop going through the motions, you begin to examine it on a deeper level and think about the context surrounding it. You relate it to other concepts or information, and you generally make sense of it below surface level.

All of this, of course, is designed to push information from your short-term memory into your long-term memory. That's why cramming or studying at the last minute isn't an effective means of learning. Very little tends to make it into long-term memory because of the lack of repetition and deeper analysis. At that point, it becomes rote memorization instead of the concept learning we discussed earlier, which is destined to fade far more quickly.

When you set out to learn something, instead of measuring the number of hours you spend on something, try instead to measure the number of times you revisit the same information after the initial learning. Make it your goal to increase the frequency of reviewing, not necessarily the duration. Both matter, but the literature on spaced repetition or distributed practice makes clear that breathing room is necessary.

It's true that this type of optimal learning takes up more time and planning than most of us are used to. However, if you find yourself short on time, you can still use it strategically.

To cram for a test, exam, or other type of evaluation, we don't need material to make it to our long-term memory. We just need it to make it slightly past our working memory and be partially encoded into our long-term memory. We don't need to be able to recall anything the day after, so it's like we only need something to stick for a few hours.

You might not be able to do true spaced repetition if you are cramming at the last minute, but you can simulate it in a small way. Instead of studying subject X for three hours only at night, seek to study it one hour each three times a day with a few hours between each exposure.

Recall that memories need time to be encoded and stick in the brain. You are doing the best imitation of spaced repetition you can with what you have available. To get the most out of your limited studying time, study something, for example, as soon as you wake up, and then review it at noon, 4:00 p.m., and 9:00 p.m. The point is to review throughout the day and get as much repetition as possible. Remember to focus on frequency rather than duration.

During the course of your repetition, make sure to study your notes out of order to see them in different contexts and encode more effectively. Also, use active recall versus passive reading. Don't be afraid to even intersperse unrelated material to reap the benefits of interleaved practice. Make sure to focus on the underlying concepts that govern the information you are learning so you can make educated guesses about what you don't remember.

Make sure that you're reciting and rehearsing new information up to the last minute before your test. Your short-term memory can hold seven items on its best day, so you might just save yourself with a piece of information that was never going to fit into your long-term memory. It's like you're juggling. It's inevitable that you'll drop everything, but it could just so happen that you're juggling something you can use. Make use of all types of memory you can consciously employ.

Spaced repetition, as you can see, approaches learning from a different perspective—in practicing retrieval and shooting for frequency as opposed to duration to improve memory. Even in situations where you don't have as much time as you'd like, you can use spaced repetition to cram for tests and overall just get more information into your brain—again, by focusing on frequency and not duration. When you spread out your learning and memorizing over a longer period of time and revisit the same material frequently, you'll be better off.

The next piece of the puzzle in better memorizing is called chunking. Unlike spaced repetition, this might be something you've heard of before, and it might even be something you currently do.

Chunking

Chunking is a memory technique you may have heard of before, and for good reason. It's important to understand, because it can drastically reduce the amount of information that you have to remember or learn. How? Because chunking is a way of looking at information—encoding information—and putting it into terms that are easier for our brains to process. The brain has natural limits, but we can be creative n the way we work around these limits, and effectively extend them.

Chunking is the act of taking multiple pieces of information and combining them into fewer pieces, which is obviously easier to memorize. Mnemonics are an example of chunking, as are acronyms. A simple example of how chunking works is to think about a telephone number. If you want to memorize a telephone number, it's difficult to commit seven independent numbers to memory. That is seven pieces of information for your brain to individually encode, store, and attempt to retrieve when you need it.

However, you could create two three-digit numbers and a single-digit number, which is actually easier for your brain to process. 1234567 would become 123-456-7. Instead of seven pieces of information, suddenly you have two or three. Now ask yourself, which method is easier? That is the power of chunking—it turns a lot of information into something that is simpler to digest and manage. And it's easy to do, because all you are doing is viewing multiple things as one, and your brain will follow suit.

A simpler example is to imagine how hard it would be to memorize a list of twenty random words. It would be much easier if those words could be strung together thematically or into a narrative. And you would probably be able to remember close to 100% of it if you put those words into a meaningful sentence. The brain is built for meaning and pattern-making – make meaningful patterns and it does its best work.

Chunking came about because of the discovery of *Miller's Magic Number 7*—a discovery made in 1956 by George Miller. He proclaimed that most people can store between five and nine pieces of information in their short-term memory, for an average of seven items, which accounts for the name.

However, what constitutes a piece of information can vary widely. Therefore, chunking information together can greatly increase what we hold in our short-term memory and make us far more effective. It's more accurate to say that we can hold five to nine *chunks* of information in our short-term memory at a time. As you might recall, short-term memory has limited capacity, and chunking serves to cram as much material inside that limited capacity as possible.

Another way to think about chunking is to create one meaningful piece of information from multiple pieces. Whatever list or set of information you are analyzing or trying to commit to memory, attempt to break it down into anywhere from five to nine pieces. This won't just make you analyze the information with a more critical eye; it will also take advantage of Miller's Magic Number 7 and feed data to your brain in a way it can handle.

How can you use chunking in your learning? Chunking is best with lists to memorize—they don't have to be of related things; you just have to be able to find a way to combine them. Earlier, we had the telephone number example of putting separate pieces of information into fewer, larger chunks. That's just a list of numbers arranged into a shorter list.

Another example is to memorize a list of things to buy at a grocery store. How can you create chunks from this? By looking for patterns and associations between the things on the list. You are chunking the information based on the overall meaning and significance. Look for what items share in common and how they can be distinguished from other items.

Suppose the things on the list are: bread, spaghetti, meat, onions, peppers, tomatoes, and garlic. At first glance, there appear to be a few categories:

-bread, spaghetti
-meat
-onions, peppers, tomatoes, garlic

By organizing the items on the list by type or category, you've created three chunks of information as opposed to a list of seven items. Three is better than seven when it comes to memorizing.

A final example is using mnemonics with the first letters of each word of the list. The letters of the shopping list we used before are: b, s, m, o, p, t, g. Can we organize that into two words that are easy to recall? What about SPOT BMG? Now you've got two chunks of information instead of seven.

Chunking allows you to know the limits of your memory and optimize your information to suit those limits. It allows you to take advantage of how our minds would prefer to function and simply reduce the amount of work you have to do. Chunking can work for just about any type of list you want to memorize; you just have to be creative and understand how the items can either be separated or grouped together. Then you can reduce the number of pieces of information you take in.

Retrieval Practice

Remember all the talk about recall being the strongest and most desirable form of retrieving memories and information?

The more active, the better, because it makes your memory participate in the process with focus. Retrieval practice is something that makes us dig deep into our memory banks and work hard mentally, but at the same time it's one of the most effective ways of truly memorizing information. Here's how it works.

We typically consider learning as something we absorb—something that goes *into* our brains: the teacher or textbook spits facts, data, equations, and words out at us, and we just sit there and collect them. It's merely accumulation—a very *passive* act.

This kind of relationship with learning returns knowledge that we don't retain for very long because, even though we *get* it, we don't *do* much with it. For best results, we have to make learning an *active* operation.

That's where retrieval practice comes into play. Instead of putting more stuff *in* our brains, retrieval practice helps us take knowledge *out* of our brains and put it to use. That's what cements memory. That seemingly small change in thinking dramatically improves our chances of retaining and remembering what we learn.

Everyone remembers flashcards from childhood days. The fronts of the cards had math equations, words, science terms, or images, and the backs had the "answer"—the solution, definition, explanation, or whatever response the student was expected to give. The idea of flashcards sprouts from this concept. This approach is neither new nor very complicated: it's simply recalling information you've already learned (the back of the flashcard) when prompted by a certain image or depiction (the front).

Retrieval practice is one of the best ways to increase your memory and fact retention. But even though its core is quite simple, actually using retrieval practice isn't as straightforward as passively using flashcards or scanning over notes we've taken. Rather, retrieval practice is an active skill: truly struggling, thinking, and processing to finally get to the point of recalling that information without clues—doing much of what we've discussed already in this book that accelerates learning.

Pooja Agarwal researched pupils taking middle school social studies over the course of a year and a half, ending in 2011. The study aimed to determine how regularly scheduled, uncounted quizzes—basically, retrieval practice exercises—benefitted the ability to learn and retain.

The class teacher didn't alter their study plan and simply instructed as normal. The students were given regular quizzes—developed by the research team—on class material with the understanding that the results would *not* count against their grades.

These quizzes only addressed about a third of the material covered by the teacher, who also had to leave the room while the quiz was being taken by the students. This was so the teacher had no knowledge of what subjects the quizzes included. During class, the teacher taught and reviewed the class as usual, without knowing which parts of the instruction were being asked on the quizzes.

The results of this study were measured during end-of-unit exams and were dramatic. Students scored one full grade level higher on the material the quizzes covered—the one-third of what the whole class included—than the questions *not* covered on the no-stakes quizzes. The mere act of being occasionally tested, with no pressure to get all the answers right to boost their overall grades, actually helped students learn better.

Agarwal's study provided insight on what kind of questions helped the most. Questions that required the student to actually recall the information from scratch yielded more success than multiple-choice questions, in which the answer could be recognized from a list, or true/false questions. The active mental effort to remember the answer, with no verbal or visual prompt, improved the students' learning and retention.

The principal benefit of retrieval practice is that it encourages an *active* exertion of effort rather than the passive seepage of external information.

If we pull concepts *out* of our brain, it's more effective than just continually trying to put concepts *in*. The learning comes from taking what's been added to our knowledge and bringing it out at a later time. We mentioned flashcards earlier and how they're an offshoot of retrieval practice. But flashcards are not, in and of themselves, the strategy: you *can* use them and still not be conducting true retrieval practice.

Many students use flashcards inactively: they see the prompt, answer it in their heads, tell themselves they know it, flip over to see the answer, and then move on to the next one. Turning this into *practice*, however, would be taking a few seconds to actually recall the answer and, at best, say the answer out loud before flipping the card over. The difference seems slight and subtle, but it's important. Students will get more advantages from flashcards by actually retrieving and vocalizing the answer before moving on. Forcing yourself into situations like using flashcards and taking practice tests is what makes you remember at your best.

In real-world situations—where there's usually not an outside teacher, premade flashcards, or other assistance—how can we repurpose what we learn for retrieval practice? One good way is to expand flashcards to make them more "interactive."

The flashcards in our grade-school experiences, for the most part, were very one-note. You can adapt the methodology of flashcards for more complex, real-world applications or self-learning by taking a new approach to what's on the back of the cards.

When you're studying material for work or class, make flashcards with concepts on the front and definitions on the back. After completing this task, make another set of cards that give "instructions" on how to reprocess the concept for a creative or real-life situation. Here's an example:

- "Rewrite this concept in only one sentence."

- "Write a movie or novel plot that demonstrates this concept."

- "Use this concept to describe a real-life event."

- "Describe the *opposite* of this concept."

The possibilities are, as they say, limitless in how you can seek retrieval. Remember, your goal is to require yourself to reach into your memory, display the information, and only then put it back.

In order to make the best use of your flashcards, commit to making two sets. The first set will contain mere definitions and single concepts:

one-word prompts for one-word or one-sentence answers.

The second set of flashcards will contain as much information about a single concept as possible so you will be forced to recall all of that with the prompt of a single word. This is also known as chunking information, where it's advantageous to your short-term memory (which can only hold on average seven items) to remember information as a large chunk rather than as smaller, individual components. This means that when you put more information on each flashcard, that set of information becomes one item versus five items.

When you go through your flashcards, put the cards you got wrong back into the middle or front of your stack so you see them sooner and more frequently. This helps you work through your mistakes and commit them to memory more quickly.

Using these exercises extracts more information about the concept that you produce yourself. Placing them in context of a creative narrative or expression will help you understand them when they come up in real life.

Retrieval practice is simple enough with flashcards and essentially testing yourself. When you make your brain sweat a little to dig the information out of your memory, you'll find that information sticks in your head extremely well. In addition to basic flashcards, get fancy and prompt for information that will test the limits of your understanding and knowledge. What's important is to keep drawing the information *out*, and your memory will greatly improve.

The next lesson of this chapter is about changing locations, and the ways that your surroundings or context are related to your memory. It's why when we smell roses or certain scents, we are reminded of times from when we were younger. Memory is contextual, and the next lesson will show you how to use that to your advantage.

Change Locations

Changing location sounds like it doesn't have anything to do with memory and learning, so how does it tie in to the rest of this chapter? Bear in mind what your brain as an organ actually evolved to do. Memory is there to help you make sense of the world and make connections – in other words to survive. The brain makes associations all the time – everything it encounters is connected in complex webs with everything else that is already known. The brain never processes isolated bits of information in a vacuum, for no reason. This means that the more context, the more variety, and more connected associations you can create, the better your memory will work.

Our memories are not just triggered when we want to recall them. They are sometimes unconsciously triggered because they are associated with everything that was present when we made that memory. That's why smells or songs can instantly transport us to another time and place. The particular smell or song was present when the memory was formed.

This technique is about the phenomenon that studying the same material in different locations and environments helps memory retention.

A study by Robert Bjork found that information is remembered and encoded into our memory holistically. This means that if you study Spain in an aquarium, your memory will associate the two subconsciously. Your memory will also associate what you wore that day, what you ate, the smells in the aquarium, and what stood out visually in your environment. They'll all be lumped together as far as your memory is concerned, along with the specific information you are trying to remember or learn.

This means two things.

First, that it is possible to evoke the memory of Spain just by being exposed to the same smells and visual stimuli. If they are part of your overall memory of the information, then they will act to remind you of the rest of it. In other words, if you studied Spain in an aquarium and see a picture of an aquarium, it's entirely possible that it will remind you of the information you learned about Spain.

Second, if you change locations frequently while learning and processing the same information, you are strengthening your memory because the material will be associated with multiple locations, smells, and general stimuli to make you remember it. The researchers deemed this increased neural scaffolding and memorization. The more stimuli that triggers that memory or information, the more deeply it is encoded in your memory like a growing web. Memory and information are contextual.

What does this mean for you? You should change locations as frequently as possible while learning the same information. If you can't change your scenery completely, change what's on your desk, the music you are listening to—anything that impacts any of your five senses. The more shifting of stimuli, the more roots the information will take to your brain.

Scientists have found other links between memories and other associations. Ruth Propper of Montclair State University found that even muscle contractions, namely a clenched right fist, could be subconsciously associated with information and memory if done simultaneously. One group of participants clenched a ball with their right fists while performing a memory task, while other groups either had no ball at all, or clenched their left fists.

The first group routinely performed the best. Why does this work? It could be similar to why changing locations increases memory retention, because the more stimuli, the more cues for the information.

Just think of these phenomena as creating more roads to the information that you want in your brain. Each time you switch locations or associate the information with something else, you build more roads for easier access and deeper encoding.

For instance, if you are studying and learning from nine a.m. to three p.m., that's six hours. You can plan to switch locations every two hours. This helps with your contextual encoding and retrieval. To take it to the next level, you can add in different temperatures, sounds, smells, and sights for each location—each of the five senses can help you make and recall memories.

To take full advantage of everything these scientific studies have demonstrated, expose yourself to different situations, locations, and contexts while studying. Split your study session into different locations and stimuli for every hour or two. Switch locations. Mix things up, and make it a habit to move around. Remember, this is what gives your information more roots to take hold in your brain and help you recall it.

Construct Vivid Imagery

Constructing vivid imagery—off the top of your head, can you guess why this helps your memory? I'll give you a simple example. When you think about your past year, what do you remember, boring things or exciting things? Undoubtedly you remember the exciting things because they made an impact on you. Think about this – are you more likely to remember a mnemonic that has a rude joke in it about someone you personally know? Or one that is neutral and kind of uninteresting?

Our cognitive powers, attention and memory are wrapped up in our emotional processing. We cannot help but pay more attention to things that are personally or emotionally meaningful, funny, scary, novel or inspiring. Abstract ideas and concepts simply don't hold the same appeal as lived reality in our senses – especially a reality that is rich and ticks emotional boxes for us. This is something we can take advantage of in our everyday quest for learning and better memory.

A large body of research indicates that visual cues help us better retrieve and remember information. The research outcomes on visual learning make complete sense when you consider that our brain is mainly an image processor (much of our sensory cortex is devoted to vision), not a word processor. In fact, the part of the brain used to process words is quite small in comparison to the part that interprets visual images.

Words are abstract and rather difficult for the brain to retain, whereas visuals are concrete and, as such, more easily remembered. To illustrate, think about your past school days of having to learn a set of new vocabulary words each week.

Now, think back to the first kiss you had or your high school prom date. Most probably, you had to put forth great effort to remember the vocabulary words. In contrast, when you were actually having your first kiss or your prom date, I bet you weren't trying to commit them to memory. Yet, you can quickly and effortlessly visualize these experiences now, even years later. You can thank your brain's amazing visual processor for your ability to easily remember life experiences. Your brain memorized these events for you automatically and without you even realizing what it was doing.

There are countless studies that have confirmed the power of visual imagery in learning. For instance, one study asked students to remember many groups of three words each, such as dog, bike, and street. Students who tried to remember the words by repeating them over and over again did poorly on recall. In comparison, students who made the effort to make visual associations with the three words, such as imagining a dog riding a bike down the street, had significantly better recall.

Based upon research outcomes, the effective use of visuals can decrease learning time, improve comprehension, enhance retrieval, and increase retention. Memory is largely visual, so we should take advantage of that.

How? Take a list of objects you want to memorize: rabbit, coffee, blanket, hair, cactus, running, mountain, tea. There are eight items.

This would seem to be incredibly difficult to memorize because everything is unrelated. However, you can give yourself a better chance by creating a vivid and striking mental image for each item. It doesn't have to be a literal representation of the word, or even related to it.

For instance, what images can you create for rabbit? You could use a mental image of a normal, cute rabbit, but that's not likely to be distinctive in your memory. You could conjure up an image of what the word rabbit makes you think of, a symbol, what the word sounds like to you, or how the word is written. The more outrageous and unusual, the better for you to memorize, because we tend to easily forget normal things.

When you put this same amount of thought into the eight items of that list, you will be able to memorize them more effectively. It's not just taking advantage of how your brain works; it's the attention and time to choosing an appropriate mental image.

When you can get into the habit of not taking information at face value, and instead going deeper, thinking about it, and constructing vivid imagery to make it stand out in your mind, you'll remember things far better. It might even be the simple act of taking the time and picking out vivid imagery that makes information stick in your brain, but whatever the case, it works.

Create a Story

Let's start this lesson with a question similar to the previous section—what do you remember better, a boring movie or an exciting movie? Of course, you remember the exciting movie better because of the impact it made on you, and in a word, it was memorable. Another question: are you more likely to remember the weird movie that you didn't understand and didn't make much sense, or the thrilling movie that had you enthralled until the conclusion?

The human brain was not built for factoids, but for meaningful narratives. Before the invention of writing, people did not consider it a great feat to recite from memory great epic poems and songs thousands of words long. Narratives are a way to encode information in a format that you brain loves best. Let's start with an illustration to immediately feel the difference a story can make.

First things first, try to memorize these words in this order: rabbit, coffee, blanket, hair, cactus, running, mountain, tea. It's the same list from the previous section.

Now, take a sheet of paper and write down the words you remember in the exact order they were listed. See how many you can remember.

Most people can remember between three to four words. If you got more than that, that's great. As you can see, relying on just your natural memory isn't the best idea. If you can get 50 percent of the items on the list, that's considered good. That's not a good baseline for learning!

Now we come to the point of this technique, which is to create a story that involves all those items. When you can create meaningful connections between items instead of trying to memorize dry facts, you stand a better chance. A story ends up being one large piece of information rather than eight distinct pieces; this is similar to what happens when you attempt to chunk information from earlier in this lesson.

By creating a story for those words, you'll be able to memorize all of them in the correct order far more easily. What kind of story might you construct with the list we have? As with the previous method, the more unusual and outrageous, the better and more memorable it will be.

As a reminder: rabbit, coffee, blanket, hair, cactus, running, mountain, tea.

It could start with a rabbit who went to jail for selling drugs hidden with coffee. He has now tried to attack his cellmates in jail by making weapons with his blanket and hair tied together. However, one day, he found a cactus while running outside in the prison yard. By trading this cactus for three kilograms of tea, he was able to escape to the mountains above the jail and was never seen again.

One item is a brain trigger that helps you remember the next item. It's similar to hearing a song where each verse brings you to remember the next verse, and you can remember all the words to a song.

The main principles of this technique are to make each item distinctive (imagination) and link it to the next one (association). The crazier you can make the story, the better. The more distinctive, the more it will stick in your mind. When you make up your story, visualize it in your head with as much color and movement as possible. Practice the story two or three times.

Then, test yourself to see how many you can remember. Like I've said before, these techniques to improve memory are so effective because they're a reflection of how memory works.

Creating a story is another way to pay close attention to your information and then have it make sense to you in a way that lets you recall it easily. The main idea is to create meaning from meaningless and unrelated facts or information, which, of course, makes it easier to remember.

Mind Mapping

Finally, we come to another visual means of assisting our memory.

I'm completely converted to the practice of mind mapping. It's a method of organizing information that highlights key concepts, relationships of elements, processes, and ideas in ways that are meaningful to us and more digestible by our brains. I use mind mapping for everything from learning about new topics, to brainstorming narratives, to organizing events, even as a diary of sorts.

Mind maps are also perfect vehicles for improving your memory. The very nature of mind maps relies on visual representations of subjects and connections—and as we now know, visuals are particularly useful in memorizing.

Creating a mind map is simple and very instinctual. Like the memory tree above, the first step is coming up with a central idea or theme: "tomato sauces," "repairing a car transmission," "British heraldry," "the Marvel Comics universe." Literally any broad subject you can think of is fine to put in the center.

From there, you draw lines as branches to subordinate subjects relating to your theme. For example, if you're working on tomato sauces, you could put out initial branches that refer to sauces of particular cuisines—"Italian," "Mexican," "Spanish," "Indian," "American," and so forth.

The idea is to keep on drawing branches that connect to the larger ideas. For example, under "Italian," you could list specific types of tomato sauces that originate from Italy: "marinara," "puttanesca," "Bolognese," "Arrabbiata," and so forth. Under each sauce, you can draw branches to specific ingredients, cooking tactics, good wine pairings—there really is no limit to what you can categorize with a mind map.

How you use text in this format is completely up to you, but the nature of mind maps encourages brevity—so they're very effective if you use keywords or short phrases, which are typically much easier to remember than long sentences.

Mind maps are great ways to use color and imagery to represent certain elements, which promote the advantages of visuals in memorizing. For example, in our Italian tomato sauce epic, you could represent Bolognese, a meat-based sauce, with clip art of ground meat in a spoon. Arrabbiata is a spicy sauce, so you could illustrate that with a chili pepper. Mnemonics in action!

The organizational aspect of mind maps is another way they can reinforce memory. Relationships, connections, hierarchies, and associations are easy to represent in a mind map. And as we just discussed, understanding relationships and associations with a certain element increases the chance that we'll remember it.

Mind maps are especially fun and effective on paper, where you can add color and images with your own hand (which is also beneficial to memory). But since I possess the drawing skills of a hermit crab, I use a mind map app. It's especially easy to reorganize your information—you can take a branch and move it wherever you want, or quickly draw lines between different branches, whatever you prefer.

The organizational and visual aspects of mind maps play right into efforts to improve memory. These maps help you literally draw a big picture, showing you how everything relates to a certain topic. That foundation is ideal for developing better recall skills.

This is the end of the chapter on memory, and it's been a long one. That's because for many people, the essence of better learning is really in understanding just how to memorize or cram information more easily and quickly.

Takeaways:

- Memory is a funny thing. It's fickle and sometimes likes to hide. But the tactics in this chapter will work hard to prevent that.
- Memory is a three-part process: encoding, storage, and retrieval. And then, to retrieve the memory itself, there are three possible ways to do it: recall, recognition, and relearn.
- Use spaced repetition and measure your rehearsal by frequency, not duration.
- Use chunking to create larger but fewer pieces of information.
- Use retrieval practice to draw information out of you, which solidifies it more firmly in your memory banks.
- Change locations, because memory is contextual, and your surroundings will factor into the memory.
- Construct vivid imagery, because what is exceptional tends to be better remembered.
- Create a story both for logical flow and to create something that is vividly memorable.
- Use mind maps for visual representations of your thoughts, and organize them neatly, to cement relationships between concepts.

Chapter 4. Paths for Gaining Expertise

We've considered strategies for finding and managing information, and we've looked at ways to boost the memory so you're making the most of this information, given the limits of your brain's processing power. But this is still not the same as having expertise. How do we convert our growing knowledge and memorized knowledge into a cohesive sense of proficiency?

Unfortunately, achieving a level of expertise isn't something for which there's an established sequence of events or plan. Being an expert is just the end destination, and there are many pathways and examples you can use to become an expert. This chapter describes some of the best ways to engage and challenge yourself, as well as strategically use your time.

The models we're going to discuss have different focuses and methods, but they all serve the same end: getting you into that rarified, exclusive 1 percent of people in a certain discipline who know or do the most. And remember: you don't have to employ all these models, and you shouldn't. You only need to choose one, and stick with it. In fact, you should get into the habit of choosing one and just going with it instead of letting analysis paralysis hold you back.

For example, let's say there are two friends who both became experts in astronomy. One obtained their expertise by following the actions and study path of a role model—a well-known astronomer whose work is easily studied and traced. The other poured through a series of books and charted their course through mind maps. These ways of getting expertise are structurally different, but they're both valid directions to take. Neither is wrong, and the best path for you is the one that *works for you*.

Follow the Leader

Consciously or not, all of us likely have a role model we've admired and respected in a certain field. A great way to start building expertise, therefore, is to follow the direction of what's more generally called an *exemplar*: a person in a given discipline who stands as a role model for you to aspire to and learn from.

Emulating the thought process, activities, and results of an exemplar helps on several levels we've discussed so far in this book: understanding the landscape of the subject area, filling in knowledge gaps, and learning what paths to take to build and refine our knowledge. Of course, we're not mindlessly aping this person, but allowing them to be a kind of remote mentor, and someone who can give us a workable framework to move forward.

You don't need to make them an official mentor, or even know them; it's enough that you have a model who took specific steps for you to try to emulate. It can be someone who you simply observe; when you learned to tie shoes as a kid, you watched how someone else did it. In fact, most of the practical things we learned as children were through observation of what our older siblings and parents did.

Exemplars are more than someone whose work we consume and admire. Remember that expertise is only the end-product – for our exemplars, we are interested in the *path* they took. We might like the destination someone arrived at, but their method for getting there may not actually work for us. We need to find a process that we wish to emulate, not an outcome. This is why so many successful people often cite strange or unrelated role-models – what appeals to them is not the outcome, but the manner in which the outcome was achieved. Through the steps and routes they've taken to become experts, they encourage us to attain their level of expertise by observing what they do and say, and adapting that information for ourselves.

Working with an exemplar over the long term is achievable through seven steps, according to Harvard professor and author Dorothy Leonard. The idea is not to merely imitate people you admire, but take what you learn from them and convert it to actionable lessons that apply to your own unique life.

1. Identify the best exemplars. Who are the leaders in your chosen area of expertise? Who are the ones who receive the most acclaim and appreciation for their particular areas of genius? Who has a starting point similar to yours who motivates you the most? Who seems to be the most attainable from where you are right now? And which of them would you most like to imitate?

It's not too difficult to find the standard-bearers in your field. They're the ones whose names crop up repeatedly in online media or television; they show up frequently in your search results. Neil deGrasse Tyson's name is all over search results in astrophysics. Konstantin Stanislavski is a hugely revered name in the study of acting. Even if they've passed on (as Stanislavski has), you should be able to find elements of their work that you can incorporate and replicate yourself. You should be able to locate ample resources online about their work and accomplishments.

Don't leave out less-famous people closer to home whom you may have easier access to: a college professor you studied under or a local business leader with name recognition around town. If you're looking to gain expertise in the restaurant field, you may have a chance to see your exemplar at work at their local businesses.

Don't discount anyone as an exemplar, and don't just seek out the so-called "famous" people in your field. You can probably think of a few famous people who got there on something other than their own merit, so be sure to weed out those who are simply lucky or privileged and focus on those you can learn something from. Often, the best exemplar will be the one who takes the most interest in you and whom you have the most access to. As they say, the best diet is the one you can adhere to. The same principle applies here.

2. Assess the gap between you and them. You won't gain your exemplar's wealth of knowledge overnight. But in some cases, it may not take as long as you may immediately think. The knowledge gap between you and a chef will almost certainly be less than the one between you and an aviation expert. What's important is to not let the distance intimidate or overwhelm you – the path from where you are to where they are is long, but it is composed of simple steps, one after the other.

Your exemplar has extensive knowledge about their subject. They've studied volumes and tallied up a considerable amount of real-world experience in their field. They speak fluently about their expertise, and they produce tangible work from that background—whether it's a book, a house, or a wedding cake.

Compare that with what you've accomplished in your field so far. How long and seriously have you studied your subject? How easily can you explain it to others? What have you produced in learning this subject? Where are the gaps in your knowledge, and how did your exemplar fill them?

Determine how much work it will take for your expertise to get to the level of your exemplar's. Be as specific as possible. If the gap is small, you should feel a lot more positive and assured about your chances. If it's large, it will take a lot more of your energy and resources to get to their level. Seriously consider whether you want to make that extended effort. Also consider if you're willing to push through adversity and challenge – which you'll find plenty of in the histories of experts!

3. Study on your own. This is where the real action begins. Particularly if the expertise gap is a big one, generate as much learning and knowledge as you can without the personal guidance of someone else. Learning on your own is a big forerunner to following the steps of your exemplars. You should see how far you can get on your own initially – many experts have done precisely that. You might surprise yourself, and you might even come up with a novel perspective of opinion that your exemplar doesn't seem to have considered.

Of course, this begins with simply knuckling down and studying the information you gather.

What else? There are online courses galore that will teach you anything from coding to world history to art appreciation to being a stand-up comedian, usually for a reasonable financial investment and sometimes for dirt cheap. You can seek out other peers closer to your level of knowledge and talk to them about what they've learned so far and where they need to go. You can also begin an intensive study of reading materials in this step, research history or news stories, or even do some casual experimenting if that's appropriate for your chosen subject. Maintain a curious, growth mindset and stay consistent, and you'll be tallying up experience that all counts towards your goal.

4. Persuade experts to share with you. If by chance you're able to establish communication with an expert at this stage, you may consider asking them for a few minutes of their time. Many would be happy to, since it's always a source of encouragement when someone asks for a few moments of their expertise. But there is a large caveat here.

You should have at least a firm base of knowledge in your topic before you engage with any *real* so-called experts. You don't want them to think they have to teach you everything from the beginning—that's a lazy form of questioning and a waste of their time. Questions are always welcome, but lazy questions will rightfully out you as someone not willing to work as hard as they have, or someone who expects easy answers given to them with a bow on top. You should have at least enough pre-existing understanding to comprehend their answers without much effort. If you're asking an English literature expert about the themes in the works of the Brontë sisters, you'd better have actually read their books.

But some experts may still be hesitant to engage you, whether they have privacy concerns or just don't have a lot of time. Before you establish contact with them, try to do a hefty amount of the legwork, both to demonstrate your seriousness to the topic and convince them that they won't have to explain everything from the beginning. And make sure they know you don't expect them to offer huge amounts of their time—keep your encounters with them as brief as you possibly can, and as easy as possible for them to say yes to even if it's just answering quick questions via e-mail. Unless *they* can't stop talking.

5. Learn to pull knowledge. A huge majority of the time, new knowledge won't be coming down from the sky and plopping itself right in front of you—you'll have to go get it. Just because you've found an exemplar or mentor you want to follow doesn't mean they're going to download everything they know into your brain. You have to figure out the best way to extract the knowledge you're seeking from them.

The exemplars you consult cannot be expected to tell you how to learn—they're not going to outline certain points, structure your learning experience, or hand you a syllabus. Even though you're seeking to be at their level in the same topic, they got their education in a different way than you are. They're coming to it from a different perspective than yours. Expecting them to frame what they have to teach you into your chosen format is only going to frustrate you both. Your knowledge and your relationship with your exemplar will both gain mightily if you make your own adventure—take what they have to give you and frame it on your own.

Don't be discouraged by the fact that you have no idea where to get started. Scout for openings and opportunities to build up your knowledge. Learn how to be a sponge that absorbs new information almost as a force of habit. Ask for examples, and put your eternal faith in the word "why?" Be proactive in asking questions, following up, and ensuring that you are not letting things slip through the cracks. Release your expectation of being spoon-fed, as we all typically are in our formal educations.

This step is hard to give instruction for because each situation and conversation is different, but think of how you might act when you are interrogating someone with a specific purpose. You would prioritize understanding and get behind the assumptions people speak with. Many experts will tell you that their big insights came from deliberately breaking with tradition or exploring areas of friction with other stablished experts. Lean into this. Make your own (intelligent) path.

6. Observe experts in action. If you've managed an in-person relationship with an expert, see if you can arrange to be a Watson to their Sherlock Holmes (as unobtrusively as you can). If they allow you to shadow them, watch closely (but unobtrusively) and observe how they resolve issues and fix problems.

When watching them work, ask yourself questions about the steps they're taking in their process. Don't interrupt them by asking them directly—instead, engage your own mind to answer why they're doing what they're doing and what the final result is. You may even come up with a way you would have approached the problem differently. You can read about something one thousand times and still not know how to apply or use it when the moment comes.

If your expert's *not* someone you've set up a personal connection with, try to find examples of their work on YouTube or other online sources.

That way, you'll have all the access and none of the urge to interrupt. This is far from a passive process, and it works on the proposal that a picture is worth a thousand words. Sometimes people process visual information more effectively; whatever the case, a demonstration will give you real-world, firsthand experience to the expertise you seek, and not just an academic, sterilized version. You can discover what experts do in the heat of the moment and why—the so-called tricks of the trade, which is not something you can glean from Internet research.

7. Seek mini-experiences. Look for "smaller" chances for encounters that your exemplar might typically experience. There will be parts of their experience that you can't access, of course. But imagine what they might be doing if they were walking the world outside their office or private chambers. The easiest way to do this is to break down what they know or do and attack it piece by piece.

If your exemplar is a master chef, for example, you could go to a local farmers' market or exotic spice shop to experience how they search for and select certain foods. If your exemplar's a musician, that gives you a good excuse to go to a music club, get close to the stage, and try to focus on how the musicians work together. Whatever you can do to raise your own awareness of their world will help.

Think of it as compartmentalizing portions of the exemplar's knowledge, and expanding on each of those compartments individually. It might be the best you can do at the moment, but it is also incredible for learning all the pieces that comprise the overarching puzzle. Eventually, you can fulfill most of the compartments that contribute to the expertise—and magically, you're an expert! Imagine working at a farmers' market, a pastry shop, a butcher's shop, a food delivery service, and a kitchen in short succession. You would have quite the repository of knowledge regarding sourcing ingredients for a restaurant. You become your own teacher, coordinating your own curriculum.

Putting all this together, let's say you're looking to build your expertise in filmmaking, and you've decided a certain film critic should be your exemplar:

> *1. Identify the best exemplars.* There are film critics all over the web and TV, but you want someone who takes the art more seriously and can teach you more about the history of film, not just the popular blockbusters—probably someone who writes about film. You eventually find a highly respected critic who has a wealth of published work, and choose him.

> *2. Assess the knowledge gap.* Reading his work, you come across the names of directors, film techniques, or genres of

cinema you're not familiar with. How often in his work does he bring up these figures and terms? How much work would it entail for you to rise to his level of knowledge?

3. Study on your own. You start studying some of the subjects the critic has brought up in his reviews—books, video interviews, and, of course, movies.

4. Persuade experts to share with you. You might consider getting in touch with the critic himself, just to ask a brief question and potentially set up a relationship. (Don't turn yourself into a pest, though.)

5. Learn how to pull knowledge. You're studying film, looking for the same elements your exemplar has, finding resources for written knowledge, and putting yourself into the routine of acquiring information about film.

6. Observe experts in action. You've shadowed a couple of film critics at film festivals and seminars just to get a sense of how they work day to day.

7. Seek a mini-experience. Perhaps you've even found a local independent filmmaker who's looking for a break, and you've offered to interview them as your film critic exemplar does. Finally, you post your final product—the completed interview—on YouTube for everyone to check out.

You've come from finding your exemplar, through understanding his work and his process, to taking his instruction and making it your own. And not once have you appeared to be a creepy stalker. Good work!

Become the Minimum Viable Expert (MVE)

Exemplars take different paths to get to their level, but there's a good chance a lot of the tools and elements experts in a certain field have used are similar among them all. A room full of master chefs might specialize in different cuisines and styles—but at some point in their learning, they all depended on the same measuring cups, knife skills, and heat sources. They all went different directions from there, but once they were all at that same basic point where they needed to master certain skills that would set them apart from their peers. At what point could they have felt or defined themselves as experts? Earlier, if they were intentional about it.

Finding out the base measure of the knowledge you need for expertise helps you construct an overall view of the field you're pursuing mastery in. It's like learning the alphabet before you can learn to read. You'll get a better feel for the landscape of the subject and what's most important about it, which will help you speed up your learning process.

This is what we can call the *minimum viable level of expertise*. It's meant to signify that sometimes, you don't need as much knowledge or skill as you think to be an expert—and in fact, if you zero in on what really moves the needle in terms of expertise, then you might just be able to sneak into expert status on the basis of a strategic collection of skills, or deep knowledge in a particular domain. After all, many experts today distinguish themselves on small differences that ultimately don't matter much. In the chef example, all competent chefs can cook you an amazing meal. Just because the cream of the crop argue about the minute details, it doesn't mean you have to – focus on creating that amazing meal and you're most of the way.

What do the top experts in your field know? What really sets them apart from others (i.e. from non-experts, not form other experts)? If you tried, you could probably break it down into a handful of aspects that, when combined, create someone to be reckoned with. That's what your aim is—to find the minimum number of important elements, focus on what matters, and get up to speed fast. You could also consider what is expressly *not* included in this minimum inventory of skills – you can often do really well in life by simply avoiding the most common and disastrous mistakes!

How much do you need to know? Perhaps not as much as you think if you are strategic about it.

Many people feel that expertise is a deep and thorough understanding of everything in a certain field. That's an impossibility, of course. Instead, define expertise as knowing enough to know where to look to solve a problem or give an educated answer to a question, which is far more applicable to the real world. Expertise is also about clearly knowing what you *don't* know – and how to identify and learn from those who do.

In becoming the minimum viable expert, let's use the example of the financial field. When considering the field, chances are a few known experts in that discipline will come to your mind.

For example, in thinking about who drives thought in the financial world, Warren Buffett immediately springs to my mind. Janet Yellen comes next. Mulling it over some more, Michael Bloomberg, Larry Fink, and Ray Dalio come up.

Imagine what you could do if you had the sum knowledge of all five of those figures. That may sound outlandish—and frankly, it is. But if you were to spend just a few hours in a room where all five of them were talking shop, chances are you'd pick up a lot.

Motivational speaker Jim Rohn famously claimed, "You are the average of the five people you spend the most time with." It's hard to refute that statement. Think back to when you were a kid or a teenager, and the five people who were always hanging around you. Undoubtedly, you picked up on some of their character, as they did with you.

What that means in the discussion of expertise is that you should avidly study the five or six experts and thought leaders in your field. At least one of them has almost certainly written a book about your subject (like *The Essays of Warren Buffett*)—go read it. More contemporary figures might produce podcasts, blogs, or websites related to their field (like mikebloomberg.com)—study them all.

When you are able to recite, describe, and understand the main principles these top thought leaders are known for, you will essentially possess a level of expertise above 99 percent of people in the world. And certainly it is enough to be considered a minimum viable level of expertise. What's more, you'll absorb the less tangible aspects, i.e. their attitude and mindset, which may in the long run prove more valuable to your success.

Start your maps. This is where mind maps work their magic. Mind maps are ways to organize information in a visual way that more closely resembles how the brain processes—by showing the relationships and order of all the various aspects of a certain topic. Think of them as freeform outlines that make whatever you're learning more relatable and memorable.

For every expert you've identified, start a mind map with their name in the center. If you happen to have found a sizable book or media of another kind, make a separate mind map covering just that book.

Then, draw branches from the center to the specific things you have learned about them—the particular expertise of that expert, so to speak. For example, if you're mapping out Warren Buffett, you might draw connections to "value investing," "stock ownership," "private equity," and "philanthropy," just to name a few. If you're mapping out a book, this step is much easier: just select chapters from the table of contents and put them on your map.

At this point, your mind map will represent a good survey of where you'll be going in your journey to expertise. In fact, it's given you a literal to-do list of what to discover and learn about. After this step, you should have at least a few separate mind maps that will likely include at least twenty-five separate items or pieces of knowledge for you to collect on your journey to expertise.

Expand your mind map to include details. Now that you've got your head down in the material, start putting in the particulars. Study the expert material and/or book thoroughly and review them several times. Fill in important keywords and essential phrases that you'll want to develop.

In our Buffett example, out of the "value investing" label you could draw bubbles labeled "undervalued stocks," "dividend yields," "future growth," and "risk management." From each of those elements, you'd make entries with other keywords pertinent to those subjects, maybe linking keywords under one label to those of another to highlight a relationship or similarity.

What started as twenty-five separate items now may have turned into over one hundred. It may sound overwhelming, but if you imagine the difference between an expert and your current level to be only understanding and applying one hundred concepts, it's not so bad.

Clean up and tighten your mind map. Brevity and clarity are the bedrock principles behind mind maps. All maps are necessarily simplifications of the terrain they are depicting, and in drawing a mind map, we're forcing ourselves to focus on the most important and fundamental aspects. Long phrases or sentences clutter the page to distraction. We're talking keywords, general concepts, and tight idioms here. Words that aren't essential to the principle thought—like "I," "we," or "the"—can be struck out.

As you go through your mind map, you might find some branches may be redundant or not as vital as you initially thought they were. Cut out branches that don't have to be there or combine repetitive branches into one. You should also begin to see where the mind maps overlap with each other at this point. That's a good sign—it indicates that you are getting a comprehensive view of the landscape of your desired topic, and nothing is being left out or falling through the cracks. It means the experts are agreeing with each other, and you are seeing where it happens.

Fill the knowledge gaps. By now, your maps should be a pretty consistent overview of your topic. But look carefully and review the material or book you're mapping out. Are there any points where you lack clarity, or certain elements that feel like they're missing?

Be as thorough as you can in this stage—in fact, it's a great idea to verbalize your questions about what's hazy or ambiguous out loud, if possible. Keep seeking out your answers. Once you find them, throw them on the map.

In our finance example, you might find that in all your work, you still haven't gotten a clear idea about bonds—maybe your exemplar wasn't particularly enthused about bonds (Warren Buffett isn't, allegedly) and you didn't get enough info to have a handle on the topic. In this case, you'd draw a new label for "bonds," start researching, and fill in the details as you get them. Rather than allowing knowledge gaps to act as weakness, you make the best of them and use them as points of potential growth.

One map to rule them all. Mind maps were designed to be easily expanded, or even just flat-out large. So, when you've finished work on all the mind maps pertaining to your subject, it's time to create one giant master mind map that contains all the most important elements from your experts, books, and other materials. I mean it: this sucker's going to be big. you might have to re-create it on a chalkboard so extensively that it looks like you are solving a case for the FBI.

On the first level of your map, enter each individual source that you've just studied. If you read a book, put the title in the center. If it was a blog, video presentation, or website, put the name or subject in the center. For each source, add between three and five of the most important facts to retain to the branch.

Once again, when you've finished this master mind map, give it a once-over and clean it up like you did a couple steps ago. This will result in a distinct, plain, and easy-to-understand map. The differences between your individual experts and sources will begin to fade, and the boundaries between them all will start to dissolve. This is a good thing—it means you're getting a more unified and organic understanding of the entire subject.

Again, this mega mind map is really your to-do list in disguise. You've successfully discovered the topics, pieces of knowledge, and concepts that underpin an expertise in the finance world, so get to work on learning about them all. In this way, you are able to hit what we call the minimum viable expert status more quickly than you would otherwise.

Really, you've just deconstructed what you need.

Abide by Bloom

So we come to the last tool or path for building expertise. It is called Bloom's taxonomy and it was created by Benjamin Bloom in 1956 (though updated in 2001) as a way to measure the academic performance of college students. It has since been a staple in academic institutions as a framework for crafting lessons that ensure a thorough comprehension in students. For our purposes, it's a literal step-by-step guideline for what is necessary to move your understanding forward.

Bloom's taxonomy essentially states that for the highest level of subject understanding (i.e. expertise), there are six sequential levels we must be able to complete. Most people will never make it through all the levels in the taxonomy, so don't let yourself fall victim to that fate. It's true that not every student needs to achieve the final level in every task for every subject, but if expertise is your goal, it's good to have an idea of what the peak looks like. The current taxonomy's levels are, from lowest to highest level of understanding, as follows:

- Remember. Retrieving, recognizing, and recalling relevant knowledge from long-term memory.
- Understand. Constructing meaning from oral, written, and graphic messages through interpreting, exemplifying, classifying, summarizing, inferring, comparing, and explaining.
- Apply. Carrying out or using a procedure for executing or implementing.
- Analyze. Breaking material into constituent parts and determining how the parts relate to one another and to an overall structure or purpose through differentiating, organizing, and attributing.
- Evaluate. Making judgments based on criteria and standards through checking and critiquing.
- Create. Putting elements together to form a coherent or functional whole; reorganizing elements into a new pattern or structure through generating, planning, or producing.

Once you hit the top level of "create," then you can be considered to have a deep grasp on a subject. You are now able to generate your own material, put forward independent analyses and contribute something novel to the field. Yet without advancing through each level of the taxonomy, you can't adequately perform the higher levels - or you can, but you'd do a rotten job! We see this illustrated in our lives every day whenever someone who doesn't have an adequate understanding of a topic seeks to evaluate it and make a judgment upon it. That's because of a failure to follow the taxonomy!

Bloom's taxonomy is a particularly useful tool to help guide and shape your learning process. It can serve as a step-by-step how to as well as a diagnostic tool if you feel that something is missing in your process. Basically, the taxonomy is a list of *how* to actively build expertise in a subject matter. It focuses on the mental processes that allow you to frame information and analyze it, each verb a kind of mental tool to grasp and manipulate new incoming data. Bloom's framework is great because it's so versatile and can be used literally anywhere. In the classroom, at work, or in designing your own systems for achieving your personal goals, this taxonomy gives you a shorthand to work with.

The entire taxonomy is predicated on the mental process of learning, which can actually be summed up quite nicely. Each task rests on the completion of the previous one. Before you can **understand** a concept, you must **remember** it. To **apply** a concept, you must first **understand** it. In order to **evaluate** a process, you must have **analyzed** it. To **create** an accurate conclusion, you must have completed a thorough **evaluation**.

The challenge is introspection and understanding where you currently fall on the taxonomy, because only then can you pinpoint what is required for you to move forward in your mastery. It's worth noting, too, that many of the tasks and activities associated with each level do overlap somewhat, and there's no reason why you can't repeat stages.

Let's dive into each element more deeply.

First, *remembering* contains elements like *listening*, *finding* information (using tools like *Googling*, perhaps) actively *memorizing* data, *bookmarking* important information to return to later, *highlighting* key points to synthesize later, and *repeating* information again and again to drill it.

This aspect is all about taking information and fixing it somehow so that you can store it and retrieve it later. If you're the kind of person who likes to make extensive bookmarks and notes about things you want to read or watch later, then you are actively remembering. You are also helping your long-term memory put down information whenever you tabulate or place information in easy-to-remember bullet points. Remembering also entails outlining key features or quotes or defining the main ideas so that you can recall the summary later on. Whenever you revise for an exam, you're using these skills.

Understanding happens whenever we engage with information more actively. Whereas remembering is about concretizing and storing information, understanding involves picking it all apart to better see how it works, like some people do to household appliances! *Categorizing* data (like we're doing here), *grouping* information into chunks, *inferring* from the data you have and *predicting* future events based on it, *summarizing*, and *paraphrasing* in different words are all cognitive operations intended to get to the deeper meaning of a set of symbols or patterns.

Teachers who ask their students to write things "in their own words" are doing so because they don't want to test for memorization; they want to test for understanding. If you comprehend a thing deeply, you are able to manipulate it, no matter how its components are rearranged or what symbols are used to express it. If you've ever tried to explain something complicated to someone who's not familiar with the concept, you may have found it helpful to give them a related example. You could outline a metaphor from a concept that they'd understand more easily and show how the ideas relate to one another. This *relating* and *associating* is key to developing deep understanding of a topic.

Applying is the third category. This is, broadly, where information is brought into the "real world" and made manifest, whether that's by *executing*, *sketching*, *acting out*, or *articulating*. As you're probably noticing, many of these terms have significant overlap with other verbs in other categories—and this should obviously be the case, when you consider that the brain isn't ever truly performing discrete activities, but rather flowing in one continuous action that, for our purposes, we're trying to understand using different models.

In fact, Bloom's verb taxonomy is itself a form of "applying"—it's *charting* or *presenting* information in a concrete way—i.e., applying the abstract concepts to make manifest a model, idea, or concept. *Painting*, *preparing*, *displaying*, *reenacting*, and even *playing* are all verbs associated with this category of the taxonomy. Every time you make a pie chart to illustrate data, turn a plan into reality, or design an experiment that actually gets carried out, you're "applying."

The fourth category is *analyzing*, which is pretty self-explanatory. Verbs in this category include *questioning*, *explaining*, *organizing*, *deconstructing, correlating*, and *calculating*. This includes all those verbs that show us actively operating on and manipulating information that comes in, not just to pass it from one form to another, but to look closely at its constituents, trying to understand them. Bloom's theory itself is an example of *appraising* and *categorizing*. You're participating in these functions when you draw a mind map, integrate one set of ideas with another set, break down a machine into its components, or ask, "Why is this happening?"

The fifth element is *evaluating*, and it includes any verbs that show that we're applying some value judgments to the material in front of us. In the previous category, analysis is value-neutral and merely about understanding. This category, however, concerns things like *criticizing*, *rating*, *reflecting, reviewing, assessing*, and *validating*. This is where our brains practice discernment—and the weighing up of the information against stated goals. How useful are the results of your experiment? What is the quality and veracity of the claims you're appraising? How well did you perform? How can you *editorialize* or else compile all this information into a whole that actually says something?

The final verb group is *creating*. Here, our relationship to information is quite fundamental: we make it! *Composing* music, *mixing* known things to create something new, *filming* a movie, *writing* the script, and *role-playing* the characters are all creative ways to engage with information and build something novel. Other creative endeavors you might not have thought of include *programming*, *designing* systems, *adapting* material from one form into another, or even things like *podcasting* or *blogging*. Interestingly, Bloom even considered *leading* to be creative, since leadership often involves guiding people toward an entirely new and self-made vision.

Again, these verbs and categories will always overlap—the point is not to identify discrete categories. Rather, this model is a tool to help you play with information and see it from many different angles, in the same way as a toolbox of differently colored glasses could be worn to look at the same information in varying lights. When you're trying to learn and memorize, it makes a huge difference to engage actively and deliberately with information—not just in one or two ways, but in as many as possible. This way, data comes alive, becoming three-dimensional and allowing you a depth of understanding that will last longer than more shallow impressions.

Whenever you're learning something new, you might, for example, highlight the text in the book so you can summarize it (remembering) and then paraphrase that text in your own words (understanding). You can then apply your understanding by constructing your own chart or diagram (applying) and taking some time to break that diagram down, questioning it, and linking it to other diagrams you've already made (analyzing). You can ask yourself after all this whether these methods are actually helping you retain the material (evaluating) and use your assessment to guide the further development of improved systems of learning (creating).

It sounds tedious, and it can be, but that's the true path to information synthesis. In fact, it's this tough mental work and struggle that really cements concepts and facts in your brain. A teacher's job is to make sure they're facilitating your learning, and Bloom's taxonomy helps ensure a smooth, comprehensive path. When you're acting as your own teacher, however, it's up to you to take note of where you are in the process, and what the next task is. If you're feeling stuck, ask yourself: what level am I on and what level comes next? Identifying the next relevant task can get you back on track and provide some focus and direction.

All these paths to becoming an expert can be helpful to you—but again, all you need is one. The approaches discussed in this chapter are just ideas – they are valuable only as far as they can be usefully applied in your actual life. Have a choice in mind before you start work on any particular model or technique, so that you have a clear path to follow and concentrate on. Then, pay attention to how it's working for you. Experts are not afraid to tweak things to suit their needs, ask questions, or challenge themselves to go beyond.

Takeaways:

- The path to expertise is not one size fits all. The endpoint is usually the same, but we all have do what works for us in getting there.

- The first path to expertise is to emulate an exemplar. This doesn't have to be an official mentor. Rather, it's someone whose path you can follow and use as a guide. To do this, you'll identify exemplars, pinpoint the gap between you and them, study on your own, attempt to consult the exemplar, observe exemplars in action, and seek your own experiences in application.

- The second path to expertise is by understanding what you need to possess the minimum viable level of expertise. This comes from realizing that once you have a high understanding of what the top few people in your chosen field espouse, your expertise will be sufficient for just about every scenario. Therefore, using mind maps, deconstruct what these thought leaders preach and break their big thoughts down into smaller and smaller concepts for you to learn. You've just created your to-do list.

- Finally, Bloom's taxonomy is a sequence of thought elements that encourage deep synthesis and different levels of expertise. In fact, each of the six phases imparts a guideline for how to interact with information more deeply to ensure comprehension. Before you can understand a concept, you must remember it. To apply a concept, you must first understand it. In order to evaluate a process, you must have analyzed it. To create an accurate conclusion, you must have completed a thorough evaluation. The challenge is introspection and understanding where you currently fall on the taxonomy, because only then can you identify what you must do to move forward.

Chapter 5. Mindset of the Expert

Expertise is about knowledge, learning, and understanding. At least, that's what you are seeking tactics to improve on. But it should be abundantly clear by now that learning is not just a cognitive phenomenon. It's an emotional, behavioral and psychological one, too. Many intelligent and talented people jeopardize their efforts because they have limiting core beliefs or bad habits that undermine their work. Luckily, there are specific and recognizable perspectives and mindsets you can adopt to maximize and focus your efforts.

Let's begin with the obvious: Actions begin with thoughts. Thus, we should ensure that we have the appropriate and most productive thoughts to aid in the actions we'll need to take in the long road to expertise.

A mindset is the mental attitude you have toward learning and gaining expertise, and this chapter contains some particularly useful thought patterns that all top-level experts possess – as well as hints to the kinds of attitudes and beliefs that will jeopardize that learning.

The first mindset to embody is the mindset of realistic expectations.

Realistic Expectations

Developing expertise, even when using the methods in this book to speed up its acquisition, is not a quick path. It's not an easy path, either; depending on what you choose to seek expertise in, it may take years. Decades, sometimes.

Put simply, if you don't understand that it can be a marathon, you won't make it very far. We need to set realistic expectations of our own skills and talents, and how they translate into gaining expertise. We also need to have realistic expectations when it comes to how quickly we can progress and advance, and simply how things will turn out in the future.

Most of the time, our expectations are too optimistic. We have an ideal picture of what we want to accomplish, usually based on seeing a perfect example of it made by someone else. There's nothing wrong with being inspired by others' success and fantasizing about big dreams, but it can't be the only thing you do. You cannot think, *Bob finished that path in just three months, so that means I can, too. Notwithstanding the fact that Bob has five years of relevant experience that I do not...*

Even though we realistically know that years of practice and work went into Bob's example, if we try to make it just once and fall short, we can sometimes feel defeated. It doesn't make a whole lot of sense, but that's often how we think. Imagine how we feel when we watch sports and feel that we could do better in some instances than professional athletes. It is unlikely, but it's a natural thought to have while sitting safe and sound on the sofa, expending zero effort!

If you have impractical hopes that you'll learn in a snap, you're going to be beset by disappointment if you lag, fall behind, or miss certain milestones. Which you definitely will. You'll slow down, and eventually you'll get so discouraged that it'll seem futile to continue. Catching up can seem like double the work, and you might just give up. After all, the bigger the expectation, the bigger the failure and fall. The larger the distance between your lofty expectations and the reality of the daily slog towards it, the more likely you are to get discouraged and give up.

As this malaise takes hold, it makes it more difficult to finish other projects—sometimes, even, with tasks we already know how to do. It also sets up comparisons in our heads that aren't fair or reasonable—you're setting yourself up for failure when you compare your worst to Bob's best, or only what he allows others to see. You can overlook all the difficult days Bob must have had, and keep focusing only on the shiny, impressive end result. You may even start to think that struggling and working hard is a sign that something is wrong, because you should find it easier. Remember the old fixed mindset? It's a recipe for giving up.

It's wise not to launch in with unachievable, out-there goals and expectations, but there's also a risk in setting ambitions that are too *low*. This is when you set a pace for yourself that is not challenging. You might do this because secretly you feel unconfident about pushing yourself, or lack faith in your abilities. You may even subtly sabotage your work but pretend that you're just being slow and steady – this can happen if we're ambivalent about our goals. The trouble is that low expectations can derail learning because you'll grow bored and you won't be engaged. You'll start to think, "Why am I even doing this? Why does this matter? This is pointless."

For example, say you want to teach yourself to master French cuisine from scratch. It's easy to come up with too-high expectations in the world of cooking. You won't instinctively know what herbs go in what dishes or in what combinations.

You're not going to make a chocolate mousse perfectly. You will not be able to make a perfect French onion soup within days of practice. In fact, it might take you a few days to even learn to cut onions correctly.

But you can also set expectations that are too *low*. You might just use canned soup for the base of your French onion soup and be done with it. You might just use the same one or two herbs for everything and call it French. Or you could just cheat on the mousse and head straight for the packaged powder you can get in the gelatin aisle. You might not *care*, in other words.

Today, it's fashionable to factor in self-care elements and be compassionate and gentle with ourselves, as well as quick to forgive setbacks. However, this doesn't mean that we have to have low standards for ourselves. Sometimes, we assume that it's a foregone conclusion that we won't do well even before we've tried, which is usually a sign of low self-esteem. In this way, we unconsciously limit ourselves by choosing tasks that are too easy or beneath us.

So what are reasonable expectations? To start out with, at least, realize you're in a learning situation and you don't have to feel pressure to master everything at once. Learn how to make broth or stock. Experiment with different herb blends for a while to find out which ones you like. Build skills in beating and folding egg whites or how to make a simple crème fraîche first. And all these expectations assume you already know how to perform basic kitchen functions—if you don't, *that's* where you start.

Set expectations according to what *you* know and *your* capabilities—this is your baseline—and don't compare yourself to others. This is the important part. Everyone starts at a different place and learns at a different pace. Starting from here, count the realistic steps from where you are to what you want to know. But this way, you can take steps to improve against your own baseline – it doesn't matter how slow you go, only keep moving, and keep making incremental steps towards what matters.

To stay motivated throughout the twenty-six miles of a marathon, you wouldn't set the expectation of a world record time, but neither would you aim for the time of a seventy-year-old woman—unless you are a seventy-year-old woman. One way to stay engaged is to think in terms of learning and improving just 1 percent at a time. Not too much, not too little, but consistent and growing. Of course, you may need to adjust this depending on your goal (1 percent better in the gym every session is impossible, for instance).

American business managers developed a method of improvement designed to help the US win World War II. It was based on the idea of continuous improvement in a thousand small ways. A manual created by the US Government advised factory supervisors to "look for hundreds of small things you can improve. Don't try to plan a whole new departmental layout—or go after a big installation of new equipment. There isn't time for these major items. Look for improvements on existing jobs with your present equipment."

After America defeated Japan and Germany in World War II using weapons and other products created in these factories operating under the small, continuous improvement philosophy, they passed the idea on to the Japanese to assist in the rebuilding efforts. The idea of small, continuous improvement caught on immediately in Japan and was named *Kaizen*.

While this idea of *Kaizen* was originally created with business improvement in mind, it is just as applicable to our efforts in attaining expertise. Aiming for small, incremental improvements on a daily basis may not seem like much initially, but they will gradually lead to the expertise you want. Focus on a 1 percent daily improvement, and that 1 percent compounds until you begin to notice improvements in your life.

The *Kaizen* method goes beyond the constant ups and downs of traditional approaches. It forces you to break down goals into small, discrete steps and tackle each step one at a time. *Kaizen* encourages you to take action, and your successes eventually snowball into bigger and bigger actions until you reach your desired goal. Don't seek drastic changes that set you up for failure. Just seek to do what you can with what you have. Aim for 1 percent better the next time around. This not only helps you improve, but it takes a lot of mental pressure off, too. You stop looking at others who have achieved some flashy end result, and focus instead on the easy, simple task improvement right in front of you, that you can make right now. Much less overwhelming, right?

You can probably learn more than 1 percent a day, but keeping in mind that you are on a long journey will keep you learning in good faith. It is better to consistently make and bank many tiny changes over time than it is to make one impressive quantum leap all at once – not least of which because the quantum leap is often just a fantasy, and not usually possible anyway!

So, maintaining realistic expectations will help you stay motivated and improve your mindset toward learning. If your expectations are too high, you will grow discouraged quickly. If they are too low, you will become bored. Stay in the middle according to your standards, your abilities, and your skills—and no one else's. That, along with simply shooting for 1 percent improvement, is the key to realistic expectations. Keep checking in with yourself – are you feeling uninspired? Bored? Overwhelmed? Take note and adjust accordingly – it's better to make minor course corrections like this early on than to give up completely.

Whether your expectations are high or low, one thing will be true: it will take some amount of work. That's the thrust of the infamous ten-thousand-hour rule put forth by researcher Anders Ericsson and popularized by author Malcolm Gladwell. Your main expectation should be that you will have to work, one way or another. Expecting quick fixes or overnight cheats is automatically an unrealistic expectation, and will only lead to disappointment.

Ericsson conducted studies on the development of expertise and established that expertise had a fairly linear relationship with the amount of practice and focus put forth. It might not feel that way on some days, though! It may not take you ten thousand hours to become an expert in your chosen field, but it also won't take a few easy afternoons, either, so adjust your expectations to match. Shoot for somewhere in the middle (okay, maybe closer to ten thousand than one thousand) and your expectations will align accordingly. One good tip is to avoid constantly measuring and tracking progress, only to get discouraged when you don't see much. Be patient, put in the work, and the results *will* come.

The next mindset for greater and quicker expertise is critical thinking.

Critical Thinking

Thinking critically is probably something you've heard of before, but it isn't clear from the name what it consists of, or how it applies to our desire to cultivate expertise.

Here's an easy definition: it's how to think logically and rationally about what's in front of you, and get a true and deep understanding about a subject. It's a type of thinking that allows you to solve problems more easily just because you are asking the right questions and determining what really matters. It accurately acknowledges that the information you need to make any type of decision will never be completely transparent and that you'll often have to go hunting for it. Therefore, it allows you to bypass your emotional reactions and decisions and overall just think smarter.

It can be as simple as asking "why" five times in a row when you previously would've only asked once and stayed on the surface—or not have asked at all. This is a brilliant technique for getting past your own assumptions, biases, inaccurate beliefs or unproductive expectations. We all have blind spots, and to achieve expert status you'll need to get comfortable facing yours head-on.

Why am I so unproductive at work? Because I have too much on my plate.

Why do you have so much on your plate? Because I keep getting tasks added onto it daily.

Why are you getting so many tasks added daily? Because I am the only one who can help.

Why are you the only one who can help? Because no one else has been trained, and our training systems are shoddy at best.

Why are our training systems so bad? Because our head trainer recently retired and no one has replaced him.

This is an elementary way of looking at critical thinking, but you can immediately see the value in learning and gaining expertise. At each stage of this critical thinking "why" chain, a different perspective appears to shed new knowledge. It was first about you being unproductive and lazy, but then it became clear that it was a systemic problem. You are gaining deeper insights into the problem. If you had stopped before reaching the next level, you wouldn't have been able to determine the cause of the problem and thus how to address it adequately. We could probably continue the "why" chain for a few more iterations, as well.

The solution we seek is not always plainly visible, and we might not even be addressing the correct problem. That's just one thing that critical thinking helps us with.

Though you should be open-minded and also humble, you should also learn to question what's in front of you – including and especially your own assumptions. Not everything is what it seems. Critical thinking means refusing to simply accept information at face value. Information has a source, has a purpose, and has consequences—what are they? This is the realm at which experts engage with material, and as a novice, it's a level of analysis you are likely ignoring. Expertise is not simply the ability to regurgitate facts; it implies a deep understanding, engagement with and analysis of that relevant knowledge.

Critical thinking is the ability to think clearly and rationally about what to do or what to believe. It includes the ability to engage in reflective and independent thinking, so you are not at the mercy of lazy assumptions, distorted and biased thinking or simply letting your emotional side run wild and control you. Someone with critical thinking skills can do the following:

- understand the connections between ideas
- identify, construct, and evaluate arguments
- detect inconsistencies and mistakes in reasoning
- solve problems systematically

- identify the relevance and importance of ideas

They can do this for information they find out in the world, as well as for their own ideas and conclusions – arguably the more difficult skill. Critical thinking is not a matter of accumulating information, or having the "right" opinion. A person with a good memory and who knows a lot of facts is not necessarily good at critical thinking. And they may not necessarily pass the mark of being an expert, either. A genuine critical thinker is able to deduce consequences from what he knows, and he knows how to make use of information to solve problems and to seek relevant sources of information to inform himself.

Critical thinking should also not be confused with being argumentative or being "critical" of other people. After all, being rebellious and contrarian just for the sake of it is just as limited and conventional as the person who blindly believes everything they're told. Although critical thinking skills can be used to expose fallacies and bad reasoning, this type of thinking can also play an important role in cooperative reasoning and constructive tasks. Critical thinking can help us acquire knowledge, improve our theories, and strengthen arguments. We can use critical thinking to enhance work processes and improve social institutions. We can also use it to generate fresh ideas, synthesize new concepts and arrive at novel solutions to old problems.

The essence of critical thinking centers not on answering questions but on questioning answers, so it involves questioning, probing, analyzing, and evaluating. What follows are some of the most important and powerful aspects of critical thinking.

You may not need to do this with everything that comes your way, but training this habit and mindset will serve you well. For instance, when you travel to some countries, you will inevitably possess the aura of a tourist, and you will inevitably attract unsolicited attention and inquiries. Inevitably, most of these people will not have good intentions. How can you know this? By looking at the context and digging beneath the surface of people's intentions. Critical thinking is the tool that protects you from these people.

Don't take anything at face value. The first step to thinking critically is to learn to evaluate what you hear, what you read, and what you decide to do. So rather than doing something because it's what you've always done or accepting what you've heard as the truth, spend some time just thinking. What's the problem? What are the possible solutions? What are the pros and cons of each? Of course, you still have to decide what to believe and what to do, but if you really evaluate things, you're likely to make a better, more-reasoned choice.

Similarly, consider the source of information. Do they have their own biases or motives? What are their perspectives, and why might that be? Analyzing where information comes from is a key part of thinking critically about it. Everyone has a reason for what they say and do, and they might not even be aware of it. But it's up to you to find it.

Do your own research. All the information that gets thrown at us on a daily basis can be overwhelming, but if you decide to take matters into your own hands, it can also be a very powerful tool. If you have a problem to solve, a decision to make, or a perspective to evaluate, get on Google and start reading about it. The more information you have, the better prepared you'll be to think things through and come up with a reasonable perspective or opinion. Don't rely on one person, because you never know what that person has relied upon. A singular view of an issue is destined to be biased.

Seek out assumptions. Most statements or assertions are based on certain assumptions. Sometimes these assumptions are explicit but are not always easy to find. For instance, a political opinion poll may assume that voters in all constituencies and supporters of all political parties are equally likely to vote. This assumption may well be in the small print of the report if one looks hard enough. Sometimes assumptions may be implicit and therefore harder to discern. For instance, a political opinion poll may assume that everyone polled is telling the truth about their likely voting intentions. This sort of assumption is unlikely to be spelled out anywhere in a report.

Similarly, question assumptions that are explicit or unconscious. For instance, are voters in all constituencies and supporters of all political parties equally likely to vote? Maybe voters in affluent constituencies or supporters of political parties in opposition are more likely to vote. Or does everyone polled tell the truth about their likely voting intentions? Maybe supporters of racist parties are reluctant to be honest about their true voting intentions.

Don't assume you're right. I know it's hard. I struggle with the stubborn desire to be right as much as the next person—because being right feels awesome. It's an ego trip almost everyone aims to take at some point or another. But assuming you're right will often put you on the wrong track when it comes to thinking critically. If you don't take in other perspectives and points of view, think them over, and compare them to your own, you really aren't doing much thinking at all—and certainly not thinking of the critical kind.

This is related to *confirmation bias*. This is when we only seek out evidence to support our own stances or opinions. We are inclined to take more notice of, and give more weight to, evidence that appears to confirm our current opinion or judgment. Conversely, we tend to neglect or reject evidence that challenges our current stance.

Try to weigh the evidence impartially and follow the evidence wherever it takes you. It is so tempting to seize on evidence that confirms one's original view or the prevailing orthodoxy and to dismiss evidence that challenges it, but one needs to be open-minded about all the evidence and equally rigorous about establishing its authenticity.

Don't jump to conclusions. Although the currently available facts may suggest a particular conclusion, other conclusions may be possible. You're doing yourself a disservice if you stop prematurely at the first thing that appears to be acceptable. It's like stopping and spending all your money at the first shop you see in a mall. Further facts may support an alternative conclusion and even invalidate the original one. Even when this is not the case, it is always helpful to have further evidence to support the original conclusion. Continue asking questions and considering alternative explanations.

Whatever the case, you are almost always working with incomplete or inaccurate information. Any conclusion you make is going to be a leap, but you can make sure it is a smaller leap rather than a bigger one.

Think about cause and effect. Correlation does not necessarily mean causation—that is, two variables often occurring together does not necessarily mean that one variable actually causes the other.

To take an easy example, when I get up from bed, the sun comes up—but there is obviously no causality. Yet some native tribes used to believe that particular rituals were essential to ensure the rising of the sun. A pattern was noticed and thus a relationship was assumed. In critical thinking, you should think about cause and effect, relationships, patterns, and what might be true if something else is true. These are known as inferences and deductions.

A deduction is where you take several statements or facts and say, "You said you went to medical school, work in a hospital, and saw a person you referred to as a 'patient.' I deduce that you are a doctor." It's an educated guess that's probably correct. An inference is less concrete. "You said you were a doctor. From that, I infer that you're intelligent, care about people, and work in a hospital."

Think of a deduction as taking a lot of information and distilling it down to one fact. An inference is the opposite: you take one fact and extrapolate it out into several inferences. Deduction is a conclusion that is required by a premise and can be shown to be logically necessary if the premise is true. Inference is starting with a conclusion and then guessing a premise that would produce that conclusion as a necessary consequence—if the premise is true. Sometimes this can work if you're Sherlock Holmes, but most of us are not. We need to take our snap judgments with a rather sizable grain of salt, although they can still be useful pieces of information in the grand scheme of things.

Overall, critical thinking will allow your learning to go to the next level because you'll have a thorough view of any issue or information. You can call it being skeptical, critical, or just being suspicious about everything at first glance.

To be honest, these aren't bad policies to live by. You don't necessarily need to stop trusting everyone or anything, but you should get into the habit of understanding that not everything is as it seems.

You Know Nothing

This is one of the most important mindsets for expertise because without it, you are closed to the process of learning itself.

This is the mindset of putting yourself in the shoes of a fresh student—in every situation. A student is willing to listen, be humble, and be open to new information and perspectives. You know nothing, and thus, you are in the position to listen without questioning (at first), and gather all perspectives and sources of potential knowledge.

When you know nothing, you are *humble*. Being willing to be humble and not look at others from a pedestal breaks down barriers that you may have put in place relating to your ego. It also helps to remove the fear, inadequacy, or other stress that sometimes comes with our encounters with the unfamiliar. Those are all things that occur when your pride and expectations get in the way. If you simply expect that *you know nothing*, imagine just how open and absorbent you might be.

Adopting this mindset shouldn't be a blow to the ego, although it initially sounds like you should subordinate yourself to others. What you're doing is not related to your ego—it's just putting yourself in a position to be able to listen to others and keep improving yourself bit by bit. The ego hates to admit it, but imagine how differently you would act if you could just state with a straight face, "I don't know anything and I'm willing to hear you out and really listen to you." Your chances of continued success run much higher with that mindset than the mindset of "I already know."

It's difficult, but using this mindset—even to the point of considering yourself a novice or amateur in something you've known about for years—is beneficial in helping you learn.

A common misconception about being an "expert"—even among experts—is that it implies you don't have to learn anything anymore. You've reached the fullest extent of knowledge possible in a given situation, and any suggestion that you could still learn more is almost insulting. You think—or feel—that you've already transcended all limitations and that there's nowhere to go but down.

However, ideally, there's not much difference between a beginner's mindset and an expert's mindset. That's because when someone decides they want to become an expert on any subject, the first thing they have to accept is that they will *never stop learning* about that subject. Long after they've established themselves as an authority, they will still be learning and discovering just how much they still don't know. An expert never stops wanting to fill in those gaps. The expert and the beginner, therefore, share an openness to new knowledge and insight.

The beginner's mindset is drawn from a Zen Buddhist concept, described as having an attitude of openness, eagerness, and lack of preconceptions when studying a subject, even when studying at an advanced level, just as a beginner in that subject would.

Every time you come across a new situation, no matter how much you think you know, reorient yourself to experiencing it as a beginner. Release all your preconceived notions or expectations about the experience. Treat it with curiosity and a sense of wonder as if you were seeing it for the first time.

Let's take an example of applying the beginner's mindset to learning how to play an instrument. What questions would you ask? Where would you even start? You wouldn't know what's important, so everything would seem significant at first. You'd probably be curious as to the limits of the instrument—first in how to not break it, and then in its overall capabilities. You'd be filled with wonder and also caution in the fear of making an error or breaking it. The impression it makes on you immediately won't be forgotten for a very long time.

Now compare how *little* you think about the same instrument when you've been playing it for even two months.

Those are the underpinnings of the beginner mindset. When you try to reprogram your mind to a blank slate and act as if you truly have no knowledge about something, knowledge will come far easier than when acting like you do through the form of extensive questioning and curiosity.

The beginner's mindset also empowers the ability to ask *dumb questions*. So-called experts rely on assumptions and their own experiences, often without further investigation. When you feel comfortable asking *dumb questions*, nothing is left up to assumptions and chance, and everything is out in the open and clarified. As a pithy example, sometimes we might forget someone's name and not want to ask them outright so as to avoid embarrassment. But this leaves a substantial blind spot. For another example, you might be learning about the process of plant photosynthesis and not understand the difference between oxygen and carbon dioxide. Don't carry on until you *do* know.

Seeing the same information from a new (but in reality, old) angle might be all you need to break through a plateau or reach an epiphany. That's the real value of the beginner's mindset. Sometimes we are so entrenched in our perspectives that it's impossible to see what we might be missing.

You can approach both new *and* familiar situations with this same principle. Next time you're driving a car, try noticing the things you would automatically do otherwise and say them out loud to yourself. Along with that, focus on what you sense when you're behind the wheel but have long since stopped paying attention to:

the ridges in the steering wheel, the glow of the dashboard odometer, or the sound of the air conditioner. Even these crushingly insignificant details could unlock and reveal some new element or impression that you've never experienced before.

The beginner's mindset requires slowing down and paying attention to what you've ignored for a long time, both out of habit and convenience.

The final aspect of giving your mind the space to expand and be open is *intellectual curiosity*. What is this? This is when you (accurately) assume that there are layers of complexity beneath every piece of knowledge or answer you might receive, and you are aggressive about finding those complexities. You want to discover a three-dimensional and nuanced view of something, so you would especially be curious about clashing issues, principles, and beliefs—particularly ones that run counter to your own.

This kind of assertive approach to discovering new information is an effective means of staying open and allowing yourself to learn while your ego is on vacation. The key is to regard everyone you know and meet as a potential spring of knowledge, someone who can tell you something you didn't know every time you encounter them. Actually, more than a spring of knowledge—a *huge* spring of *fascinating* knowledge. And it's up to you to extract that knowledge from them and get to the root of things, rather than stay at surface level.

The intellectually curious person does not stop pursuing the answer to the question "why?" They don't settle for the standard and banal answers they get from banal questions—they get deeper and more exact until they've uncovered the ultimate root and foundation of the topic they're investigating. They assume there are multiple levels of complexity in everything, and they're eager to discover what those levels are.

This is a mindset but also a habit you will need to cultivate. It's not easy to simply *desire* to do the tedious work of digging deep, especially if people aren't as willing as you to engage. But the assumption of complexity and underlying forces is undoubtedly a key to deep and accelerated expertise.

The ways to become more intellectually curious may seem obvious at first glance. If a topic rouses your interest, follow it relentlessly through reading, research, and answering your own questions. Engage with people in the field you're most interested in, and never be afraid of asking a dumb question. Embrace your state of not knowing as an advantage rather than a handicap.

Security expert George Treverton suggests that a good way to approach the unknown is as a "mystery" as opposed to a "puzzle" like a crossword or jigsaw. "Puzzles may be more satisfying, but the world increasingly offers us mysteries," Treverton wrote in *Smithsonian* magazine. "Treating them as puzzles is like trying to solve the unsolvable—an impossible challenge. But approaching them as mysteries may make us more comfortable with the uncertainties of our age."

To further cultivate the habit, author Philip Dow suggests taking ten minutes a day—an almost ridiculously easy time commitment—to dive into a topic or subject that interests you but you haven't had the time to learn about yet.

How differently would you act if ego and pride weren't in your way? You'd feel absolute freedom to pursue your curiosities down deep rabbit holes.

The final aspect of the mindset that you actually know nothing might be a harsh truth to some, but hopefully it relieves most of you: *you are a work in progress and always will be.* You will experience monumental changes in the way you think, feel, and behave over long periods of time. You may even be a legitimate expert in multiple disciplines. But you will, unfortunately, never *quite* be there—at least, this is the mindset you should embrace.

It's not that you won't accomplish great things or shouldn't show some pride in your achievements. It's just that you *can't stop* there.

There's always more to pursue, so you can't rest on your laurels and stop learning.

Albert Einstein published his theory of general relativity—arguably the most significant scientific moment of the twentieth century—in 1915. He could have stopped right there and cemented his legacy forever. But he continued to refine his theory throughout the next decade and a half, incorporating information about electromagnetism and finally updating his findings with the theory of distant parallelism in 1929.

I suggest a change in your mindset of self-identification: the elimination of the phrase *"I am"* and the adoption of the phrase *"I'm working on it."*

When you say "I am," you're immediately giving yourself a label that acts more like a to-do list: "I am lazy," "I am stupid," and so on. You've crystallized that belief and made it part of you, and thus, that's how you will act. That makes change so much harder. If you really *are* lazy, the "I am" statement has boxed you in that corner and branded itself to you.

But by changing that statement to reflect what you want to *become*, you've flipped the momentum. Instead of saying "I'm lazy," say *"I'm working on being more productive."* Instead of saying "I'm stupid," say *"I'm working on improving my knowledge and study skills."*

Instead of saying "I'm unstable," say *"I'm working on* knowing my triggers and how to react more evenly."

And of course, instead of saying "I'm an expert on medieval horse breeding," you can change it to *"I'm working on* becoming an expert on medieval horse breeding." It is a completely different sentiment with a completely different set of actions and behaviors.

This way of thinking also keeps you in line with the humility aspect of the learning mindset if you flip it toward your positive traits. Instead of saying "I'm smart," try saying *"I'm working on* being smart." Instead of saying "I'm talented," say *"I'm working on* developing my talents." You're not saying you're *not* smart or talented. You're saying you're working on improving yourself—which can and should be an unending process.

In turn, this viewpoint might increase your enthusiasm for learning and discovering new things rather than stunting your enthusiasm with the idea that you already know it all. We need to take a beginner's mindset in learning, because it allows us to put aside our egos and notice things we have since grown accustomed to. We also need to embody intellectual curiosity and get into the habit of pursuing our interests. Finally, we've learned that we are always works in progress, which simply means that whatever your current level, you can't stop there.

In addition, a beginner also seeks feedback to right his or her course whenever possible.

Swift, specific and accurate feedback is essential to continued expertise, and it is not easy to get. Imagine practicing anything physical, such as throwing darts, for example, but blindfolded. Since you have no idea how accurate each throw is, you have no feedback on how to improve, and your progress is likely to be limited. Now imagine that after practicing darts blindfolded for six months you get a report on your progress. Perhaps this is better than nothing, but not optimal. Sooner is better, and the more honest and harsh, the better. The goal is accurate and precise expertise, not good feelings and incomplete understanding.

How can you get the feedback you need to progress? One traditional source of feedback is a coach, whether official or not. If you can find people you trust to give you accurate criticism, treasure and encourage them. The other source of feedback is "real world" feedback from your environment, and generally consequences from your actions. If you are a teacher, you can get immediate feedback on how effectively you have explained a concept, by asking your student to explain back to you what you have just taught them. If you are a manager, you can gain knowledge on how well you have motivated a team member, by observing the change in their performance. Whatever you are learning, you can put it into application and see how your assumptions and understanding fare.

The One Problem with Expertise …

Everyone wants to build expertise. But what if honing specialist knowledge and skill could actually act against you in some ways? This book would not be complete without an honest appraisal of the dark side of expertise. If you've ever encountered a stubborn, know-it-all expert who simply could not admit that they were wrong, you can probably guess what this blind spot is.

Enter the *Einstellung effect* (German for "setting" or "attitude"), which explains why boosting expertise can inadvertently reduce your creative problem-solving skills, and overall trap you in a prison of your own knowledge. Nobody would argue that developing niche expertise is a waste; however, this expertise can also act as a burden and hindrance. If, as an expert, you rely on the knowledge and experience you already have, you are at a distinct disadvantage wherever novelty of thought is called for. Have you ever seen a layperson offer a more creative or intelligent solution to a problem than all the so-called experts? This effect could explain why. If you know exactly how something should and usually does play out, then it's hard to break out of this type of fixed thinking.

This is especially true if you continue to use outdated concepts simply out of habit. Just because something has worked for years, it doesn't mean it will continue to work, and thinking so has the opportunity cost of missing out on beneficial new information. The research actually shows that practiced expertise hampers creative problem solving in some instances. Accumulated knowledge is a wonderful thing, but it's also stiff and rigid, and less liable to respond fluidly in the moment. Experts may cling to an idea of a classic and obvious solution so tightly that they fail to see the better solution staring them in the face. On the other hand those who embrace the "beginner's mind" may be flexible, alert and humble enough to respond in better ways to emerging challenges that experts cannot.

The Einstellung effect was first described in 1942 by Luchins and Luchins, who had study participants conduct a water jar experiment, amongst many other variations. They asked them to measure out a specific quantity of water using a series of three jars of different capacities. One group was allowed to try out the task and arrive at a formula that would solve the problem. The other group didn't participate in this round. Both groups were then given a similar task, but where the solution was quite simple; the group who had already gained expertise of the formula unsurprisingly tried to apply it again, missing the simpler solution—which the second group, with no practice or experience, found more easily.

This shows us that prior knowledge can act as a preconceived solution that can actively block a better solution from being discovered. Counterintuitively, the first group were the "experts," but performed worse because of it. It certainly makes you reconsider all those experts in the world keen to tell us how things should be done! Knowing this about the Einstellung effect, and knowing that experts often charge more for their services, you can ask whether some problems in your life could be better solved by more creative (and cheaper!) non-experts.

Follow-up research has showed similar results with creativity puzzles that non-experts seem to fare better with. Karl Duncker's famous Candle Problem showed that when people had preconceived ideas about how tools should be used (in this case, a box of matches, a candle and some thumb tacks) they failed to find unconventional solutions (mounting the candle on the wall by using the match box as a ledge rather than lighting the candle with the matches). What the participants already knew actively prevented them from seeing what was in front of them, and learning anything new.

Practicing certain solutions puts you in a mind state ("Einstellung") to apply that same solution again rather than seek novel solutions.

Interestingly, when the researchers hinted to participants to think outside the box, they found the solution more easily, suggesting that deliberately questioning your expertise can help moderate the Einstellung effect. It might be merely a question of becoming aware of knee-jerk ways of thinking. Another method to lessen these priming effects is to change the way in which information is presented or absorbed. Hints, clues or rearranging elements can be enough to loosen old conceptions and allow a novel solution to be felt. Try reframing a verbal problem in visual terms, reorder information, or literally change the position from which you're viewing something.

A related concept is "functional fixedness"—this is the rigidity that accompanies how we think about certain tools or the right way to solve certain kinds of known problems. Again, it comes from expertise and a knowledge set that appears to be deep with predictable expectations. Creative solutions often depend on looking at old tools and concepts and thinking of them in fresh ways—or rather, removing your limited expectations of them based on the past. Children are the perfect example of non-experts since they have so little accumulated expertise and really do see much of the world as it is, rather than through old formulaic solutions and expectations.

So, how can you use knowledge of this effect in your own life? The key is in recognizing when and where it could take effect, and deliberately questioning your expertise when it leaps in to solve problems for you. Adopt a learning, open-ended mindset and be genuinely curious about what you *aren't* seeing, and what you don't understand. Try to rearrange the elements of the problem in front of you—the unfamiliarity will help support a more creative appraisal. Don't be too quick to grab hold of an apparent solution, as it can be hard to dislodge from your mind once it's there.

If you find yourself facing quite complicated new problems that ordinary expertise is not helping to solve, take a step back and think about what you would normally never do—and do that, because that is essentially the non-expert approach and perspective that you might need. An engineer might encounter a challenge in a project and find that none of the standard approaches is helping to illuminate a simple way forward. Instead of consulting her peers, she asks a junior draftsman in the firm to give their impression of the problem, and then reframes the situation in many different ways.

She even takes literal actions to clear her desk, sit back in her seat, start with a blank sheet of paper and ask from scratch, What do I know here? What don't I know? What assumptions am I making, and are they correct? She finds that the more she looks at the problem as though it's *not* an instance of the kind of difficulty she's solved before, the more she can start to unpick the details productively. She may even discover that her unconscious mind solves the problem for her in the shower the next morning.

As long as you're an expert in anything, you're going to train your brain one way or another in very stereotyped solution-styles, literally wiring the synapses of your brain to prioritize habitual ways of thinking. The best way to moderate the downsides of this expertise is simply to make room for unconscious, unexpected and truly creative possibilities in your world. Constantly remind yourself to stay in a state of learning and absorption, and don't be too quick to jump into familiar old approaches. After all, you can always turn your expertise back on once you've gained a more immediate insight into a problem. At the very least, a second and third non-expert opinion can do wonders for problem-solving.

Question expertise in the world and, most importantly, in yourself. Make no assumptions—not even about the extent to which this effect may be at play! Reframe the "givens" in any problem, look more closely at your theories and prioritize alternative perspectives. The level of expertise is found to be non-linearly related to the Einstellung effect, and non-experts can experience it as well. You may discover that even greater expertise allows you to pull back from a problem sufficiently to consider it with curiosity and freshness again.

Takeaways:

- Mindsets and thoughts belie our actions. Therefore, the mindsets and thought patterns we have toward learning and knowledge become extremely important in our pursuit of expertise.
- The first mindset is to create realistic expectations. Too high and you become too discouraged; too low and you become disengaged. The best way to approach this is to set a baseline personal to you (and no one else), and then aim for a 1 percent improvement every day—in the Japanese style of *Kaizen*. Expertise is not built in a single day, and the more you know, the more you realize that you do not know.
- The second mindset is to become a critical thinker. Critical thinking is simply not accepting things at face value. This causes you to question assumptions and motives, and overall attempt to understand knowledge and topics beneath surface value. It can be as simple as asking "why" five times in a row, not making assumptions, or thinking about cause and effect. The end result is that you think skeptically and don't accept knowledge blindly. Experts utilize this method because they know a subject matter is never so simple as it seems.

- The third and final mindset for accelerated expertise is that *you know nothing*. This isn't an insult or a challenge. Rather, it's a call to remove your pride and ego from the equation (the mindset of "I already know this") and allow yourself to learn and be taught by others. Any moment that you assume you know something is a moment you are closing yourself to knowledge.
- Closely associated with this is the beginner's mindset and how it enables you to view knowledge from new (but in reality, old) perspectives. Intellectual curiosity is also a related mindset, where you make the assumption that there are levels of complexity you must discover. Finally, accept that you are a perpetual work-in-progress and never a finished product. This simple change in phrasing can greatly affect your actions and behaviors. Overall, these are ways of thinking about knowledge that open your mind and allow you to truly listen.
- You might be surprised to know that there is actually one drawback to expertise: it can reduce your problem-solving skills in your field of expertise. Expertise is a result of experience and knowledge, which result in thought processes that are essentially cemented. This in itself is limiting, because it means you are habitualized to think in certain way that may be detrimental. Expertise creates a form of functional fixedness, where you are unable to view

other perspectives because certain principles are too hard to ignore.

Chapter 6. Expertise Rears Its Head

Becoming an expert is a little more abstract in nature than building a skill. Any how-to book for developing knowledge, such as this handy guide, probably won't have instructions as explicit as, say, a car repair manual. Sometimes with expertise, it's not *one thing* you can necessarily point out—it's a feeling of confidence and mastery when you are thrust into certain situations. It's an ineffable feeling of competence and control in the face of a task that you have slowly gathered concrete experience in dealing with.

That's why we're taking a deeper look into the various ways expertise rears its head in this chapter. First, we'll begin with analyzing two specific domains and how they can assist with expertise. Each of these fields has two important lessons each that we've yet to dive into. Combined with what we have talked about thus far, hopefully you'll be able to make your expertise-building more methodical and efficient so you never have to doubt yourself.

After that, we'll talk about two underrated uses of expertise, and how they can make life easier for you or perhaps more difficult for your rivals. In all these instances, we can see that expertise rears its head in unexpected and surprising ways at times.

Learning a Language

As we mentioned in an earlier chapter, learning to speak a foreign language puts an adult back into an elementary phase of learning. You have to contend with words and possibly letters that mean nothing to you at first. For those who have always taken for granted the ability to communicate, this feeling can be alienating and uncomfortable. It is especially difficult since we don't have all the time in the world to learn this language, unlike the native tongue we've been working on since birth, and progress can be slow and painful. Ways to make learning a new language more effective and less time-consuming are always welcome.

There are two strategies for learning a new language that can be applied to your chosen area of expertise: the 80/20 Rule and understanding the basic landscape before specifics. These concepts help you clarify the most crucial and meaningful elements in your given subject, and help you understand the best pathway to accelerate your expertise.

The 80/20 Rule. Also known as the Pareto Principle or "the law of the vital few," the 80/20 Rule has been adapted and redesigned for a surprisingly large number of applications in business and education. You've probably heard of this before.

The original rule, which was formed in the context of economics, stated that in any given endeavor, 80 percent of consequences stem from 20 percent of the causes. The principle has evolved into a versatile formula to support the elimination of excess work. For example, Microsoft claimed that 80 percent of all software crashes could be solved only by fixing the most commonly reported 20 percent of bugs. In sports training, the rule has been used to explain that only 20 percent of all exercises have 80 percent of the total health impact on an athlete. It's often said that 80 percent of the work in an office is performed by 20 percent of the employees, and so on. The conclusion, of course, is that you might as well focus most of your efforts on that impactful 20%.

In language-learning, the 80/20 Rule states that 80 percent of all conversation contains only 20 percent of all the words in a given language. As you might expect, the 80/20 Rule in language-learning supports the idea that if you maintain a heavy focus on learning that 20 percent of words, you'll have most of what you need to say covered. In fact, you could probably get by remarkably well on far less than you think (look at Randall Munroe's humorous "Thing Explainer" book, where he shows that even complex physical and mathematical phenomena can be conveyed using just 100 basic words).

For example, language expert Gabriel Wyner says that when you're beginning to learn a new language, focus only on the thousand or so most common words in that language first: "After one thousand words, you'll know 70 percent of the words in any average text, and two thousand words provide you with 80 percent text coverage."

Wyner explains the imbalance even further. Let's say you knew only ten English words: "the," "(to) be," "of," "and," "a," "to," "in," "he," "have," and "it." If that was the extent of your vocabulary, how much of any text would you recognize?

According to Dr. Paul Nation, the answer is 23.7 percent. Those ten words represent 0.00004 percent of the English language, which has over 250,000 words. But we use those ten so often that they regularly make up nearly 25 percent of every sentence we write.

Let's say we eventually increase our vocabulary to a whopping one hundred words—including "year," "(to) see," "(to) give," "then," "most," "great," "(to) think," and "there." With that number, Dr. Nation says we'd have the ability to understand 49 percent of every sentence uttered.

Let that sink in a bit—with only one hundred words, we can recognize nearly half the content of every sentence. Let's be generous and fluff his numbers—that would still mean that with two hundred words, we could recognize 40 percent of the content in each sentence. The fact that *less than one ten-thousandth* of all English words make up almost half of every sentence is kind of a big deal. That is a staggering demonstration of the Pareto Principle.

Dr. Alexander Arguelles, another polyglot working in linguistics at the Regional Language Centre of the South East Asian Ministers of Education Organization, breaks it down even further. Arguelles says that every day, the number of words every single speaker of a given language uses is 750. Furthermore, only 2,500 words are needed for you to express anything you could possibly want to say. (Although some expressions might be a little awkward or strange, 2,500 words are technically all you need.)

With that in mind, learning a language should follow that progression. Start with the one hundred most common words in a language. Focus on learning the building blocks of everyday conversation. This is the part where you should master "the," "of," "and," "it," "he," "she," "up," "down," and so forth. Words like "spatula" and "incinerator" will just have to wait.

Then, focus on becoming conversational. Wyner's research determined that those one hundred most common words in any language make up 50 percent of total spoken communication. The one thousand most common words comprise 80 percent of all conversation, and the three thousand most common make encompass a whopping *99 percent of all conversation.* (As of right now, the three thousandth most common word in American English is "lungs.") So, the next step in language-learning is not to learn more words, but to concentrate on conversing instead. The words will come through that practice. You can see that the bulk of your newfound expertise can be accelerated if you focus on the paths that are most often treaded, so to speak.

Understand the basics before the specifics. In learning a language, it's advantageous to take a large view of the landscape before embarking on the more exact nuts and bolts. The idea here is to create a context for your overall learning—to understand the outer structures and framework before actually going into the building. This is exactly the way we learnt language as babies. Some of the strategies here might include:

Figure out pronunciation patterns. As a general rule, it is always easier to memorize and grasp patterns and algorithms than individual instances (remember chunking?). For instance, certain pronunciations in French utilize more nasality than anything in English. Some Spanish words call for a roll of the "r" sound that doesn't figure in common English pronunciations. Any given language in the world has consonant and vowel sounds that no other language has. Studying these patterns gives you an idea of what you'll be learning more specifically.

Listen to an array of languages and know the stereotypes and characteristics of the one you want to learn, and gain the ability to distinguish them simply based on rough sound. Hopefully you can start to uncover the distinct speech rhythms. After you get a feel for the language's basic sound, you would move on to learning correct pronunciation for your own speech—how the words come out of your mouth.

Learn the grammar. When we speak English, we generally put a modifier before a noun: "That's a red hen." But in other languages, they order their words in reverse, so the literal translation would be "That's a hen red." So it's a good idea to understand the differences in the grammatical structure of another language before one learns the words "red" and "hen."

Watch foreign movies with subtitles. This gives you a very helpful sense of how language is spoken in practice, and will increase your overall perception of the sounds of the language of the movie. You'll hear where the rises and falls of speaking tones take place, how the rhythm of syllables sounds among people who use the language every day. You can match up the sounds, words, and speech rhythms to actual meaning. And best of all, you'll know what the heck they're talking about.

What can we apply from these lessons in learning a language for our own personal area of expertise?

Start off by mastering the basics. In building expertise, you'll undoubtedly have a lot of options on what to learn, and from your vantage point, you might not have a clear idea where to start. As with the 80/20 Rule, focusing on a smaller number of topics that have greater influence over a larger part of the general idea will help you build a solid foundation for increasing your expertise. It's likely that understanding certain concepts will provide you enough of a framework to make educated guesses on most everything else you might come across.

So, in your planning, learn about the most universal and commonly studied aspects first. If you're learning US history, you'll focus on major events that shaped the landscape: wars, economics, civil rights, political leaders, maybe a few others. Sure, you *could* study major sports events, the popularity of action figures, and the fishing industry—but right at first? No. They're of peripheral importance at best. When you understand the general landscape of economics and warfare, you can probably guess how each element flows from them.

Then develop familiarity on the most common principles. Once again, it's important to understand the basic landscape of the field to establish a strong context for your learning, which makes expertise easier to attain. What components of your field of expertise are the most relevant to your understanding as a whole? Get well-acquainted with the aspects you're more likely to refer to every day. In our US history example, that could mean focusing on the free-market system, the principles of democracy, the two-party system, and the evolution of foreign policy. It probably *wouldn't*—at this point—cover specific regions of the United States, specialized industries, or pop culture.

After putting it in context, branch out. When you've gotten completely conversant on the basics and attained full understanding of the more relevant guiding principles, that's when you can start looking at more specific branches of your interest, using your foundational knowledge as a reference point. So, for US history, this is the point where you can start learning about the Appalachian Trail, the rise and fall of the automotive industry in Detroit, how Hurricane Katrina reshaped the Gulf Coast, and so on.

Learning a Musical Instrument

Being a language expert is admirable, but there's also a lot we can understand about expertise from learning how to play a musical instrument. There's a pretty good chance that you took some kind of music class when you were a kid, by choice or by your parents' insistence. (Hopefully, you weren't scarred too much if it was the latter.) Quite a few principles common in music education can effectively help you when you're building expertise—so if you're not playing anymore, rejoice that those violin lessons weren't wasted!

I'll briefly outline a couple of the more common doctrines in learning music that translate well to becoming an expert in any field (not to mention that they're useful if your chosen area of expertise happens to be an instrument).

Go slower than you think you need to. One of the most frustrating things about learning a musical instrument is when we can't replicate a piece of music exactly the way we first heard it played, especially when it's at a quick tempo. This is the same thing that happens when we focus on the amazing end product and then get tripped up by the boring, less-than-glamorous reality fright in front of us. We sit back and wonder how guitar or piano virtuosos can play a quick line and make it seem so easy. But when we try it on our own, we can't come anywhere close to that speed without the result sounding like so much mush. Well, the experts didn't learn it at that speed, of course.

They learned it note by note, and their early practices sounded excruciatingly slow and boring – just like yours will! Thus, a particularly effective method to increasing your musical proficiency is rehearsing a given piece slowly. I mean *really* slowly. I'm talking glacially slow. Anywhere from half the normal speed all the way down to 20 or even 10 percent of the pace.

The great Russian composer and pianist Sergei Rachmaninoff—whose work is frequently impossibly fast—was known to rehearse pieces by Chopin (who wasn't exactly a speed demon) at a virtually slow crawl, taking as much as five seconds to complete a single beat. Comedian and musician Steve Martin taught himself how to play banjo by playing along with bluegrass singles on a record player that he slowed down to 16 rpm, about one third their normal speed.

There are several benefits to playing slow. It's a good way to wrap your head (and hands) around a new piece of music, by building up fingers' muscle memory, developing accuracy, and fixing errors. It also builds patience and discipline. And it reinforces the memory strategy of chunking: you're taking each part of the song apart bit by bit, concentrating only on a small portion for a slightly more extended period of time. Playing slowly helps you understand the inversions and note changes at a more meaningful level, so you'll know how to get the most out of each note when you speed it up.

The biggest benefit is that it's not only practice that makes perfect—*perfect practice makes perfect*. Learning how to play something wrong or not breaking things down only creates bad habits for you to dig yourself out of. You're effectively doubling your work if you don't go slowly.

The lesson other aspiring experts can learn from slow playing, I'm guessing, is pretty clear: slow down your pace of learning as much as you can. If your goal is to build expertise, take as much time as you need to fully grasp each concept bit by bit. It's absolutely fine to pause for meditation after a certain segment so you can grasp it fully before moving on to the next. In the analytical stage of reading (from a previous chapter) it's completely fair to read at a decidedly slower pace than normal. Fully absorb everything before moving on, because that's how knowledge sticks in your brain—the right knowledge that isn't muddled or blurry.

A slow-learning strategy helps you fully understand and remember each individual fragment that you're studying. This is an expertise that you're building for a lifetime, so you're under no rush to finish it in under a minute. It also gives you a moment to actually feel a sense of achievement and confidence. It can be encouraging to watch that effort is rewarded, and that you are making progress, even if small.

Focus on trouble spots. Researchers at the University of Texas in Austin conducted a study in practice behaviors using a group of seventeen piano majors. They told each player to learn a somewhat involved three-bar section of a certain piece. (A three-bar phrase is, for pretty much any piece of music, a *very* short segment, perhaps eight seconds long.) Each pianist was given a warm-up period, after which they were allowed to practice the section for as long as they needed. Some pianists took nearly an hour to practice the three measures; one was finished after less than ten minutes.

After they were done practicing, researchers instructed the pianists not to practice the passage again for the next twenty-four hours, even at home or from memory. When they came back the next day, they were all asked to play the passage all the way through fifteen times, only being allowed to pause briefly between each rep. The researchers then evaluated how each pianist did and ranked them all from best to worst.

With both their results and their notes from the practice sessions in hand, the researchers made some intriguing discoveries. Most surprising was that the quality of performance *wasn't* related to how long or how repeatedly the pianists practiced the music. Pianists who practiced for forty-five minutes weren't necessarily better than those who only did so for fifteen minutes.

In reviewing video of their practice sessions, the researchers made observations about the players whose performances were ranked the highest. The top three pianists, in their view, *all* used the exact same three practice strategies:

• They identified exactly where each of their errors was happening and focused on correcting them;

• They played in varying tempos throughout their practice time: slowly to fix mistakes, and more quickly to test themselves;

• They repeated certain passages over and over until they had fixed the mistakes.

What's striking about these strategies is not only that the top three pianists shared all of them, but that the majority of the other fourteen students employed no more than *one* of them, if any at all. Only two of the bottom fourteen pianists used more than one of the strategies—and *they* finished in fourth and sixth place, which wasn't too shabby, all things considered.

The three strategies that the top three pianists used all had one thing in common: they very specifically involved how the pianists managed to correct their mistakes. They didn't necessarily come to the practice session as superior players who made fewer mistakes at the beginning—they made errors. What separated them from the rest and made their performances better was exactly *how* they addressed their slip-ups.

There was one sub-strategy that the top three all employed as well—take a wild guess what it was. That's right: *slowing their playing way down*, particularly at whatever spot in the passage was giving them the most trouble.

So what does this mean for building your expertise?

For one thing, it means that having better abilities is *not* necessarily a factor in becoming an expert. It's not a matter of how perfectly you can do something from the get-go, or whether or not you're more naturally talented. It doesn't mean you have to do everything perfectly.

The difference is how you pay attention to mistakes. And this speaks to the idea of being patient, allowing yourself to stay on a certain topic that you haven't quite understood fully. Speed-reading won't win you any prizes (unless you're in a speed-reading competition, of course), and by just blowing through your study material, you may not be giving yourself the best chance to learn. Go slowly and be thorough, because that's where real understanding comes from. If you attempt to rush, you'll inevitably end up with self-created knowledge gaps that could be damaging.

When you reach a part in your study that isn't quite connecting with you, stay with it and work on it until it does. In our handy US history example, if you don't feel like you understand the cause of World War I, stick with the topic, ask yourself "why?" if you must, and keep concentrating on it until you're finally able to put all the puzzle pieces together in your mind. Then and only then can you move on to studying the specific battles of World War I, or whatever topic comes up next. Often, pieces of knowledge stack upon each other and are interrelated. If you rush through one stage, you'll have a shaky foundation of knowledge.

If you find difficult patches uncomfortable, boring or challenging, you may be tempted to escape them or rush over them in favor of the more rewarding sections you already know how to do. But, if you recall from our section on spaced repetition, practicing what you already understand may make you feel good, but it won't make you any better.

Every single one of the strategies we've talked about (in both learning language and music) all refer back to one common element: *patience*. Becoming an expert isn't something you can do on a tight schedule or with the barest of effort; it's going to take many stretches of concentrated attention to details, concepts, and changing how you think. If you can sweat through the early parts of learning where the clock seems to be moving at a crawl, you'll be amply rewarded with a new expertise. And it might not take as long as you fear.

Undoubtedly, similar types of techniques can be gleaned from the top levels of just about every discipline. I want to turn the focus from learning techniques to another way in which expertise rears its head—in perception of expertise, both good and bad. In other words, now that you've got all this expertise, what are you supposed to do with it? How do you burnish your newfound proficiency out in the wild world?

There are several ways to make your expertise productive, and not all of them involve publishing in academic journals or becoming a go-to guest on TV panel discussions. Indeed, not all of them even involve being a real expert! Expertise in itself is not so useful, is it? It's only when others know that we are experts, and a demand is created for us and our knowledge, that we are able to leverage what we've learned. Expertise is the currency for many people's careers, and it works because others see them as such.

The question thus becomes: how can you appear to be an expert and let others know?

Look Like an Expert

One of the best things about being an expert is that it's so much easier for you to actually *resemble* an expert. It's true! In just a few quick lessons, you, too, can appear to be a world-class brainiac and master of intellect! Call now and you'll receive a turtleneck sweater absolutely free! It sounds like it would fit in right along with late-night infomercials for rotisserie ovens and making passive income by working at home.

Well, okay. There are better reasons for becoming an expert than just dressing the part. And strictly speaking, you don't have to be anything close to an expert to just resemble one. But creating the *perception* among others that you're an expert has some fringe benefits. Imagine that you truly are a world-class expert but have no way of letting other people know— this is your in. Of course, this technique can be abused in a plethora of ways, but it's undeniable that appearing to be an expert can be massively useful. There's a weird reinforcement that happens, too – when you convince others of your expertise, they have a tendency to expect it from us, and we may find ourselves magically stepping up to their expectations.

Author Tim Ferriss, the self-help guru with a curious passion for getting things done in four hours, once offered a game plan for becoming an expert in four short weeks. Well—not really *being* an expert, but *looking* like one. Ferriss's suggestions include joining professional trade associations, reading some books, giving seminars, and writing for trade publications. All of which are neat things to do, but Ferriss's approach is more about keeping up appearances than *being* an expert. Remember that a big part of expertise and mastery is the psychological side of feeling confident in your abilities.

However, Ferriss says he's not encouraging people to be something they aren't. Rather, he wants people to put themselves in the most advantageous situations and present themselves in the best light. That's not off base. True experts sometimes need a little assistance in finding opportunities to display their brilliance, and that involves knowing how to present themselves to the rest of the public. It's not "fake it till you make it" but rather that faking it helps you make it a little more quickly. After all, every expert has to start somewhere. Ferriss recommends the following:

- Join two or three related trade organizations.

- Read the three top-selling books on your topic.

- Give one free one-to-three-hour seminar at the closest well-known university.

- Give two free seminars at branches of well-known companies.

- Offer to write one or two articles for trade magazines.

- Join ProfNet—a service that journalists use to find experts to quote for articles

Ferriss's ideas aren't bad at all, and the overall concept is to generate the perception of expertise by sheer name recognition and prolificness, but not all of his tactics necessarily create the appearance of an expert. The last four do—if you, the new expert, have some realistic way to convince universities, companies, and trade magazines that they need your services. Trade organizations are relatively exclusive to the people within them and are good for getting info, but they don't mean much to the outside world. And though you should always read books forever, generally people don't notice what you're reading unless you put it on Goodreads—so how does that make you appear like an expert?

To make yourself more well-known and acclaimed as an expert, follow two more specific objectives:

Go where you're needed. Self-promotion is like all other forms of advertising: it's based on finding the right market and flooding it with your image. Your expertise is now part of your image. So your directive is to find where someone with your expertise would be needed or wanted, and make yourself a universal and popular presence. Once there, hold yourself with confidence.

Ask yourself: what are the markets for your expertise? What places are receptive to your kind of abilities, talents, and know-how? Where are the people who would appreciate and need you? And how do you make yourself so well-known that you're practically unavoidable?

These places are not all physical, of course. The web is full of open-ended sites that thrive on outside contributions from well-heeled experts, and it's easy to build a presence on sites like Quora.com that constantly have opportunities for real and supposed experts.

Publishing platforms like Medium.com make it possible for you to expound on your intellect and help find you an audience. Ferriss's suggestion of joining ProfNet, a service that links topical experts with journalists needing information for news articles, is a good idea. If you turn yourself into a pervasive presence in these forums and hopefully gain a little bit of fame, you'll find yourself attracting followers and building a reputation. Find the top five forums, whether physical or not, and build a name for yourself there either by contributing, assisting, organizing, or just plain being there. Rinse and repeat for a few weeks or months, and the effect will be complete.

Who is in all the places that a particular topic is discussed? Why, only an expert, of course. The people who are omnipresent in the everyday physics field—Stephen Hawking and Neil deGrasse Tyson—are who we associate with heavy expertise. A word of warning, however - splashing your image all over the web will backfire if you don't follow it up with genuine value. These days, the barrier to entry online is virtually nonexistent, and you don't want to be perceived as blowing your own trumpet without cause.

Go where the people who matter to you are. To look like an expert, there's no better way than to be seen around other experts. With the right approach and appropriate networking skills, you can leverage your "brand" with the audiences of other experts to increase your own following, especially if they're ubiquitous on social media.

So ask yourself where other experts in your field travel, gather, or even just hang out. Conferences and conventions are excellent places to start. For virtually every profession, discipline, and field of interest, there's a convention somewhere in the world. They attract experts who are eager to build on their knowledge, learn new trends, and—very importantly—make connections and networks with other experts. If you meet just a few new experts at one of these shindigs, it could bring about great advantages.

On a more local and less expensive level, there might be a college or university near where you reside. If it has some departments and resources relating to your field of interest, it might be worth it to keep an eye out for events or meetups on campus. And once again, the web is of great assistance in finding communities of like-minded individuals.

For example, let's say you've become an expert on salt mining. You've attained enough knowledge that you've written a few blog posts on the subject. You legitimately know more than 99 percent of the world because of how much time you've spent on the topic. You've started a Medium.com account, published your informative articles there, and used keywords in the subject headings to build a little following. You post on a regular basis, which is a surefire way to build your audience. And every once in a while, you hit Quora.com and answer users' posted questions about salt mining. Your upvotes are off the charts, and eventually people begin to seek you out.

You go to a few local forums about salt mining. You make yourself a presence there, asking great questions at the panels and showing off your pre-existing knowledge (maybe once or twice asking a question you already know the answer to, just to rub it in). You present yourself as an intellect not to be trifled with, so they keep asking you back and eventually ask you to be in the panel yourself.

Then you hit a worldwide salt mining conference in New York City. You hit it off at mixers with other experts. You drop knowledge bombs and appear to fit right in. You find a few people to discuss current issues in salt mining, agree to exchange contact info and Twitter accounts, and build up your network. After the conference, you engage in discussions (and/or heated but civil debates) with these experts online, exposing you to all their followers and increasing your presence. You keep in contact with them, eventually collaborating on studies and research projects.

Well, it's hard to argue that you are not an expert at this point. In fact, you probably fit the bill and perception after the first couple steps in the process. You now look like an expert, whether you are or not. Might be a little expensive with all the travel, but honestly, it isn't that hard to appear to be an expert, is it?

Just keep in mind *why* you're doing all this—it's not just to increase your public image but to put forward your expertise. Many people only *appear* to be experts: They've done the minimum they need to convince those with limited attention spans that they're experts, but in reality, they've only gotten the look down; they can't walk the walk. If they're ever found out, the fallout may very well be disastrous. Keep that potential danger in mind if you ever find yourself focusing more on what you look like and less on what you have to offer.

Catch Others Pretending to Be Experts

For every true expert in our world (and especially on the Internet), there's at least one imposter *pretending* to have a deep level of knowledge about a subject. They might be ignorant about their lack of expertise and simply aren't even aware they're faking it. Still, others know they're not qualified and are trying to pull a con on the rest of the world. You are now in a position to catch these poseurs and bring them to justice, or at least call them out in the comments section.

How can someone *not know* they're not experts? They could simply have an inflated sense of their abilities or importance. They're driven by their egos, tell themselves (and everyone else) they're great, and therefore sincerely believe they're geniuses and never allow themselves to be questioned about it. They may not be malevolent, or may not be consciously *trying* to fool people, but they are still extremely dangerous to society.

Others may simply be too ignorant to know they're ignorant. Enter the *Dunning-Kruger Effect*.

That sounds like a harsh statement, but there's actually a valid scientific explanation for the condition. The Dunning-Kruger Effect is named after two social psychologists who ran an investigative study in 1999. Their research found that people with very low cognitive abilities—those with bad grammar, faulty logic, and no sense of humor—often believe they're far more intelligent than they actually are.

The Dunning-Kruger Effect is kind of like a vicious cycle of the ignorant. People who suffer from it simply don't have the mental aptitude to understand that they don't have the mental aptitude. This Molotov cocktail of bad self-knowledge and low intelligence makes them exaggerate and embellish their own competency. They're also unable to comprehend the intelligence and capabilities of people other than themselves. In essence, they are incapable of understanding what they don't understand.

You see the Dunning-Kruger Effect far more frequently than you might think. The self-appointed guru in a bar who spouts inane nonsense about a given topic. The tipsy uncle at a family holiday gathering who unloads about a subject he knows nothing about and declares that any opinion that opposes his is idiotic and incorrect.

Hearing these kinds of people is aggravating, galling, and a little depressing. They're not trying to fool you, but they might be masquerading as experts.

Confirmation bias. Inadvertent non-experts might also be suffering from confirmation bias, which we covered earlier. They only see whatever they want to see, and only approve information if it confirms what they want to believe is true. Their understanding is clouded by this delusion, which leads them to stop considering new data or insight the second it disproves their cherished belief.

To be fair, most of us probably operate under some kind of confirmation bias from time to time. We can't be truly unbiased about certain situations or problems, and only consider information that certifies our preconceptions and makes us happy. Doing so turns us into slaves to our opinions.

For example, let's talk about the *Illuminati*. Some insist that secret societies are real and that they're controlling everything from our water supply to our television viewing. To them, the Illuminati might represent a way to explain certain things that have happened, so they really want to believe it's true. When presented with evidence that contradicts their claims, they'll probably insist "you're just one of them" or "they *got you too*, huh?" Meanwhile, they'll swallow up any new YouTube video with crazy claims and doctored photos that shows inarguable *proof* that the Illuminati exists beyond all reasonable doubt.

That's confirmation bias in action. Of course, I *would* say that, being part of the Illuminati.

How to Nail 'Em. Whether they're aware of their fakery, whether they suffer from Dunning-Kruger Effect or confirmation bias, or whether they're doing their shenanigans on purpose, fake experts are poisoning the well of knowledge by deceiving others and misinforming the public. It may not be possible in this era to eradicate the spread of false expertise.

But we can still recognize it and call them out, simply by keeping in mind the differences between real and false experts. And, while of course *you* wouldn't dream of having any biases, it pays to know about bias anyway, not primarily to catch out fakers, but to guard against it in yourself. Here are warning signs in both ourselves and others that you might want to keep an eye on...

Real experts focus on their subject area—fakers focus on themselves. A real expert takes pride and satisfaction in the work they produce. A false expert takes pride in their own ego and usually makes themselves the hero of every story they tell. For example, a real music expert would talk about a new artist they've discovered with great enthusiasm. A fake expert would probably claim they heard them first. The focus is on making themselves to be some certain adjective, versus the music itself. Of course, there can be overlap here, but ask where your expert in question's source of pride comes from.

Real experts admit when they don't know something. A true expert is neither timid nor ashamed about admitting the limits of their knowledge. They're not embarrassed about not knowing what they don't know. They're secure. The fake expert cannot even handle the idea that they don't know everything. A true science expert would freely admit if they didn't fully comprehend the idea of game theory, while a fake expert would become defensive, make excuses, and mock others: "I know a lot of things. Unlike you." Upon further questioning, the fake expert would probably grow indignant and withdraw from the interaction.

Real experts display intellectual honesty. A real expert welcomes data, proof, or viewpoints that might refute their own findings. They seek to encourage civil discourse and thoughtful debate; they don't want to squash them. They know what confirmation bias is, and actively try to avoid it. If the evidence says something, they will change their opinion to include it. After all, they are seeking truth and knowledge, not defending a particular viewpoint. They might even search out dissent and play devil's advocate to ensure that there are no holes in their opinions or stances.

A fake expert will shut down opposing opinions and will insist that only *they* "have the truth—listen to me and me alone." For example, a real political science expert would gladly accept and hear out someone who had differing opinions on what segments of the voting public have more effect on national elections. A fake expert would shut them down and tell them they didn't know jack about politics, and that the fake expert's opinion is the only one that matters.

Real experts know when to improvise and how to do it. Sudden changes in routine don't rattle a real expert. If a surprise throws their original game plan out the window, they can come up with quick solutions and still work well. A fake expert freaks out when they're booted from their happy place. A great example of this is the television show *Chopped*, where contestants are provided a basket of unknown and sometimes mysterious food to concoct meals with. The key is that they aren't pretenders, and know enough to work within the bounds of what they are given. They can at the very least make educated guesses as to what flavors and foods will go well together.

The champions are able to navigate foreign and novel dishes with ease. If a fake expert were even allowed on the set, they'd go ballistic and the excuses would start coming. One can appear to be an expert on a very narrow line of questioning, but if the discussion goes off topic, all pretense will be lost. The ability to improvise comes from a deep understanding of first principles and how everything is connected.

Takeaways:

- Expertise is many things. But one thing is sure: everyone wants it. This fact hasn't changed throughout the course of the book. This chapter presents a few interesting ways that expertise rears its head in daily life.

- First, we have two disciplines in which expertise follows specific patterns that we can use for ourselves. Language learning involves two patterns: the 80/20 of words that matter in daily life, and understanding the basic landscape and boundaries before getting more specific. Learning to play a musical instrument likewise follows two patterns: learning and practicing extremely slowly, and not being afraid to devote time and effort to specific problem areas.

- Aside from the lessons we can glean from different disciplines, we also talk about how to create the perception of expertise. After all, expertise in itself is purely for self-indulgence; expertise is valuable when it is known and in demand. We can follow bits of Tim Ferriss's method of offering yourself to trade organizations and in-person meetups. Generally, the idea is to become relatively omnipresent in the places that matter to your audience, and around other experts. What type of person interacts with other experts and also appears to be prominent and widespread? Only an expert!

- On a related note, it's important to be able to discover when others have real or false expertise. Some people may not be trying to fool you; they just might be suffering from the Dunning-Kruger Effect or confirmation bias. But in every field, there are those who simply want to get ahead by talking the talk. You can uncover these people with a few simple questions. Are they focused on themselves or the subject area? Do they have trouble admitting that they don't know something? Are they intellectually honest? Do they know enough to improvise and make educated guesses?

Summary Guide

CHAPTER 1. ACCELERATE YOUR EXPERTISE

- Expertise can be achieved and thought of in many ways, but one of the big obstacles you may have to overcome is the myth of innate talent and how it relates to the fixed versus growth mindset.
- The myth of innate talent is that only certain people have enough talent to become experts—not true. This can be further supported by noting the differences between the fixed mindset (I can't improve) versus the growth mindset (I can improve). Whatever you put your efforts toward, you can learn and grow expertise in. It's not that you just have to use "the power of belief" or something ephemeral like that, it's just a linear equation requiring effort and time.
- The biology of expertise is surprisingly simple. Think of the brain like a muscle, and it becomes clearer. Learning and expertise take hold largely because of an increase of myelin, a fatty acid that covers neurons and

increases the speed and strength of electrical impulses—i.e., thoughts.
- Being flesh and blood, the brain has the same requirements as a bicep or hamstring. This means the presence of stress (both chronic and acute), the quality and amount of sleep, and the frequency of exercise have large effects on just how effectively you can learn.

CHAPTER 2. HOW TO FIND, INTAKE, AND UNDERSTAND INFO BETTER AND FASTER

- Expertise is built on information. That's an understatement! Gathering, understanding, and using information is what allows you to brand yourself as an expert; without it, you are just an imposter. This chapter is focused on how to effectively gather information and analyze it for deeper meaning. First, you build your inventory, and then you learn how to use everything you've got.

- This largely comes in the form of the five steps of effective research, and the different types of reading as put forth by Mortimer Adler (as well as the related SQ3R method).

- Effective research is composed of: gathering without discrimination, analyzing your sources, searching for patterns, finding the dissenting opinions, and putting it all together. This allows you to gain sophistication and nuance as opposed to shallow opinions built on anecdotes. Most of us only get halfway through the third step.

- Effective reading comes through understanding the four types of reading and how to make it through all four types to gain expertise. The four types are: elementary, inspectional, analytical, and syntopical. Again, most of us only get halfway through the third step.

- Finally, the SQ3R method for extracting information from a resource. Use it. It stands for survey, question, read, recite, review. This is not just a process for attacking a book, but rather a plan for tackling entire disciplines and fields—and whatever you are trying to learn for yourself. Most people will use some elements of the SQ3R method, such as the read and review portion, but without the other elements, deeper comprehension is rarer and more difficult.

CHAPTER 3. UNLIMITED MEMORY

- Memory is a funny thing. It's fickle and sometimes likes to hide. But the tactics in this chapter will work hard to prevent that.
- Memory is a three-part process: encoding, storage, and retrieval. And then, to retrieve

the memory itself, there are three possible ways to do it: recall, recognition, and relearn.
- Use spaced repetition and measure your rehearsal by frequency, not duration.
- Use chunking to create larger but fewer pieces of information.
- Use retrieval practice to draw information out of you, which solidifies it more firmly in your memory banks.
- Change locations, because memory is contextual, and your surroundings will factor into the memory.
- Construct vivid imagery, because what is exceptional tends to be better remembered.
- Create a story both for logical flow and to create something that is vividly memorable.
- Use mind maps for visual representations of your thoughts, and organize them neatly, to cement relationships between concepts.

CHAPTER 4. PATHS FOR GAINING EXPERTISE

- The path to expertise is not one size fits all. The endpoint is usually the same, but we all have do what works for us in getting there.

- The first path to expertise is to emulate an exemplar. This doesn't have to be an official mentor. Rather, it's someone whose path you can follow and use as a guide. To do this, you'll identify exemplars, pinpoint the gap between you and them, study on your own, attempt to consult the exemplar, observe exemplars in action, and seek your own experiences in application.

- The second path to expertise is by understanding what you need to possess the minimum viable level of expertise. This comes from realizing that once you have a high understanding of what the top few people in your chosen field espouse, your expertise will be sufficient for just about every scenario. Therefore, using mind maps, deconstruct what these thought leaders preach and break their big thoughts down into smaller and smaller concepts for you to learn. You've just created your to-do list.

- Finally, Bloom's taxonomy is a sequence of thought elements that encourage deep synthesis and different levels of expertise. In fact, each of the six phases imparts a guideline for how to interact with information more deeply to ensure comprehension. Before you can understand a concept, you must remember it. To apply a concept, you must first understand it. In order to evaluate a process, you must have analyzed it. To create an accurate conclusion, you must have completed a thorough evaluation. The challenge is introspection and understanding where you currently fall on the taxonomy, because only then can you identify what you must do to move forward.

CHAPTER 5. MINDSET OF THE EXPERT

- Mindsets and thoughts belie our actions. Therefore, the mindsets and thought patterns we have toward learning and knowledge become extremely important in our pursuit of expertise.
- The first mindset is to create realistic expectations. Too high and you become too discouraged; too low and you become disengaged. The best way to approach this is to set a baseline personal to you (and no one else), and then aim for a 1 percent improvement every day—in the Japanese style of *Kaizen*. Expertise is not built in a single day, and the more you know, the more you realize that you do not know.
- The second mindset is to become a critical thinker. Critical thinking is simply not accepting things at face value. This causes you to question assumptions and motives, and overall attempt to understand knowledge and topics beneath surface value. It can be as simple as asking "why" five times in a row, not making assumptions, or thinking about cause and effect. The end

result is that you think skeptically and don't accept knowledge blindly. Experts utilize this method because they know a subject matter is never so simple as it seems.

- The third and final mindset for accelerated expertise is that *you know nothing*. This isn't an insult or a challenge. Rather, it's a call to remove your pride and ego from the equation (the mindset of "I already know this") and allow yourself to learn and be taught by others. Any moment that you assume you know something is a moment you are closing yourself to knowledge.
- Closely associated with this is the beginner's mindset and how it enables you to view knowledge from new (but in reality, old) perspectives. Intellectual curiosity is also a related mindset, where you make the assumption that there are levels of complexity you must discover. Finally, accept that you are a perpetual work-in-progress and never a finished product. This simple change in phrasing can greatly affect your actions and behaviors. Overall, these are ways of thinking about knowledge that open your mind and allow you to truly listen.
- You might be surprised to know that there is actually one drawback to expertise: it can reduce your problem-solving skills in your field of expertise. Expertise is a result of experience and knowledge, which result in thought processes that are essentially cemented. This in itself is limiting, because it

means you are habitualized to think in certain way that may be detrimental. Expertise creates a form of functional fixedness, where you are unable to view other perspectives because certain principles are too hard to ignore.

CHAPTER 6. EXPERTISE REARS ITS HEAD

- Expertise is many things. But one thing is sure: everyone wants it. This fact hasn't changed throughout the course of the book. This chapter presents a few interesting ways that expertise rears its head in daily life.

- First, we have two disciplines in which expertise follows specific patterns that we can use for ourselves. Language learning involves two patterns: the 80/20 of words that matter in daily life, and understanding the basic landscape and boundaries before getting more specific. Learning to play a musical instrument likewise follows two patterns: learning and practicing extremely slowly, and not being afraid to devote time and effort to specific problem areas.

- Aside from the lessons we can glean from different disciplines, we also talk about how to create the perception of expertise. After all, expertise in itself is purely for self-

...dulgence; expertise is valuable when it is known and in demand. We can follow bits of Tim Ferriss's method of offering yourself to trade organizations and in-person meetups. Generally, the idea is to become relatively omnipresent in the places that matter to your audience, and around other experts. What type of person interacts with other experts and also appears to be prominent and widespread? Only an expert!

- On a related note, it's important to be able to discover when others have real or false expertise. Some people may not be trying to fool you; they just might be suffering from the Dunning-Kruger Effect or confirmation bias. But in every field, there are those who simply want to get ahead by talking the talk. You can uncover these people with a few simple questions. Are they focused on themselves or the subject area? Do they have trouble admitting that they don't know something? Are they intellectually honest? Do they know enough to improvise and make educated guesses?

www.ingramcontent.com/pod-product-compliance
Lightning Source LLC
Chambersburg PA
CBHW020527080526
44583CB00013B/773